Commercial Property and Residential Development Made Simple

How to Supercharge your Residential Property Capital Growth and Cash Flow

Andrew Crossley

First published by Busybird Publishing 2019

ISBN 978-1-925830-77-4

Ebook 978-1-925830-79-8

Cover design: Working Type Studio

Layout and typesetting: Busybird Publishing

The development diagrams supplied by Lateral Building Design

busybird publishing

Busybird Publishing
2/118 Para Road
Montmorency, Victoria
Australia 3094

www.busybird.com.au

Disclaimer

The content of this book – including its strategies, ideas, concepts, explanations, definitions and opinions – do not constitute legal, financial, property, credit, compliance, or any other type of advice. All information is general in nature. Everyone's personal situation is different and expert advice must be sought in each case from a suitability-qualified individual. You will realise that this book has not taken into account your personal situation, goals, attempts at fact-finding, your risk profile, or a multitude of other factors. This book is for educational purposes and provides no warranties as to the up-to-date nature of the information contained. Risks are involved with all investments, so you must seek appropriate advice before making any decision; we disclaim all liability for any decision you may make.

I have taken every reasonable effort to ensure the accuracy of the contents in this book; however, we do not warrant or make any undertakings as to the completeness or accuracy of any information provided. Neither I nor anyone involved in this book accepts responsibility for any action that you take as a result of the motivation or education that you will hopefully receive from this book.

Contents

Acknowledgements

I would like to thank the following wonderful people for their contributions, adding additional and invaluable scope and depth to my book: Craig Hemer (Sargeants Conveyancing), Mike Eden (Eden Lawyers), Jonathan Gan (Bluehive), John and Donna Harding-Smith (Lateral Building Design), and Harvey Bowlt (Bowlt Commercial Lawyers).

Preface

There are many strategies and choices an investor can consider and make when investing in property within Australia. My previous books have delved heavily into residential property, whilst at the same time they have covered topics with relevance to all situations.

The common theme I come across is that investors have more success if they seek guidance and they often fail when they try to go it alone.

What you gain from this book, book number five in the *Made Simple* series (and a specific accompaniment to book number four, *The 100K Property Plan*), will be similar to being mentored about what to do when thinking about buying a commercial investment property, and also what to consider to massively reduce risk and improve potential with every property purchase. Every successful investor has a plan and they follow it. They take action to implement it, and they have a team to continually advise them.

A smart investor will not just focus on capital growth; the risk of this approach is they become a slave to the cost of debt from their portfolio, and have to keep working just to make repayments to feed the negatively geared nature of a capital growth focus portfolio. They could have sleepless nights if interest rates go up, or if one or two of their properties are vacant. An intelligent investor will not just focus on positive cash flow either, as they will likely achieve less capital growth over time and, therefore, less wealth in the future. They may have less 'growing equity' in their properties to use towards future purchases. A smart investor will consider several strategies, including buy and hold, development, and subdivision, and will investigate commercial property as well as residential.

Too many authors and other professionals promote only one strategy, such as capital growth in blue chip suburbs, positive cash flow in regional locations, residential property over commercial, or buy and hold over manufacturing more growth or cash flow. Of course, the best solution is to buy a capital growth property with excellent cash flow, enhanced by the opportunity to manufacture more growth and cash flow within the property, in blue chip suburbs near major infrastructure hubs (preferably near the Melbourne or Sydney CBDs). This is difficult to do. Rarely, if ever, can you find a positive cash flow property with great capital growth potential, near Sydney or Melbourne, within an affordable, typical budget.

The reality is that not everyone can afford to buy a capital growth property at blue chip suburb prices, then spend up to one million dollars redeveloping it. The idealists out there, who promote only buying in blue chip suburbs or only buying capital growth focused properties, are just that: idealists, not realists. Their logic is perfect, in theory, but it is disconnected from the reality of the vast majority of society.

Investing with capital growth as a focus will provide a better outcome, more wealth, and a more secure retirement. This is undisputed and anyone who thinks differently is misguided. However, most investors do not earn enough to afford five to seven properties in blue chip suburbs without regard for cash flow. Most 'would be' investors do not earn 250K or more each year. They do not necessarily rate their job stability as ten out of ten, they have some fear or trepidation, and require help to invest in a practical fashion which suits them and their specific needs, not an ideological single strategy.

The obvious start is budget, loan approval, choosing a strategy, and research, then finding a location, the type of property, and finalising the purchase contract.

Having the right team around you is the most important thing you can do.

If you understand the importance of

- *not trusting a real estate agent representing the seller or a property marketing company which also represents the seller (developer) when buying a property*
- *learning to appreciate the benefit of a buyer's agent, and the invaluable reduction in risk that could be achieved by using a property advisor*
- *learning how to properly research an area to live in or to invest in*

then this book has been worth its weight in gold many times over.

Most people understand they should invest towards their future, whether by purchasing a property to live in or an investment property, just to get a foothold in the property market. Unfortunately, too many people seem to think their superannuation will provide adequate income for them in retirement, while some people think there is always tomorrow. Waiting and procrastinating can be your downfall.

There is always a reason not to invest. The perceived risk of things like another global financial crisis, the property bubble bursting, removal of negative gearing, and interest rates rising scares potential investors away, yet property just keeps on rising in value over time. It is more expensive now than ten years ago, and prices ten years ago were higher than twenty years ago. This is true of every good location in Australia. Every society is full of clowns, misfits, and irrational naysayers.

The choice is yours. If you want to know more about reducing risk and improving potential, then read on. If you do not, or you think you know enough, then put the book down. I wish you luck. You are going to need it.

About this Book

This book covers all things commercial: what to consider if buying a property to operate a business from, or buying a commercial property to lease out. It delves into development, subdivision, and how to improve a property. It may not just be residential property that you are interested in, so buying commercial property, what is involved, and relevant finance options are covered in great detail.

While it is important to have a financially secure retirement, it is also about reaching a point in life, before retirement age, where you can have more choices to reduce your working hours, quit your job, or travel. It is about having hope, waking up every day, knowing you are doing everything you can to change your life for the better. Manufacturing cash flow and capital growth can potentially help you reach your goal quicker than sitting on a property for twenty years will.

Whilst daily routine is good for most of us, it can be a comfort blanket we rely on. Having several routines other than just getting up, going to work, eating dinner, putting the kids to bed, and taking kids to their sports and activities is so important. It gives us hope that there is more out there that we may be able to accomplish.

Within the commercial or industrial industries, very wealthy investors may own the premises where they run their business (often, wealthy people are self-employed). They may own some offices, or be involved in joint ventures with petrol stations, childcare centres, and aged care facilities or retirement villages.

Commercial property is an important asset class within the asset sphere of property, so this book covers the many important considerations in relation to commercial property. These include, but are not limited to: capital growth, yield, necessary size of a deposit, what to consider when renting versus buying a premises for your business, different types of commercial property, and typical finance options.

A successful investor's residential portfolio may typically contain their principal place of residence, a holiday house or short-term holiday let, and potentially a couple of well-positioned properties in the capital cities down the eastern seaboard of Australia. Remember, these investors are not successful because they were born with more knowledge; it is because they have advisors and they have a plan.

Many people have the dilemma of deciding whether to move to another property, or to undertake an extension on their current property. Development, subdivisions, renovating for profit, building two or more dwellings on a block, and all the positives and risks associated with these invaluable strategies are explored within this book. These are some of the best strategies to incorporate in any property portfolio, but can be riskier and more time-consuming, so I have included information to guide you through this process and on what you need to know to save money and manufacture capital growth and cash flow.

Signing a purchase contract and what to look out for is so important, as well as the traps to avoid when negotiating on and buying a property. The considerations involved in the decision to renovate, develop, or subdivide your property, and what you need to know to save money and manufacture capital growth and cash flow are included.

Some people, after reading this book, will get excited for a day or a week, similar to what happens after attending a seminar or reading a self-help book, only to become distracted and entrenched back into the routine of life once again. Some people are not, and will not be, in a position to achieve their goals, maybe due to the inability to borrow money, too much debt, too many kids, not having enough money saved, not having enough interest in property, or not being goal-orientated or focused on the future. But, if I can make a difference with this book, and either save some people from themselves, or help others take the next step towards buying a property by not only having followed the information in this book, but also having sought advice from a qualified professional, then that is fantastic. I will have made a difference and that is all I can ask for.

At some point in the future you will stop work and still need income. The level of income you receive then depends entirely on you, your needs, your commitment to yourself and your family, and, very importantly, your ability to act on the commitment you have made. Most of us want more and want what is best, but may not know how to go about it, so this book will help you. Your level of success does not determine your commitment to your family, but your level of effort towards considering the future does.

The question you need to be honest with yourself about is: do you have the knowledge or experience to do everything yourself?

To build, or start to build, a property portfolio in as much of a stress-free manner as possible, I recommend you always refer back to this book, and have a team of professionals around you. This excludes a real estate agent and/or property marketing company. If you wish to have further assistance, because you do not have time to do it yourself, or you are concerned about doing it yourself, I recommend you contact me at www.Australianpropertyadvisorygroup.com.au (APAG) to work with you each step of the way.

There is a six-step process in developing a property investment plan. This is what my blueprint is all about. This book is written about Steps 3 and 6; specifically, about the buying process. It is a 'how to' guide to supercharge your commercial property capital growth and cash flow. This book also covers invaluable research tips about property development, signing a purchase contract, and the finance and settlement process.

Other Books by Andrew Crossley

Property Investing Made Simple

www.propertyinvestingmadesimple.com.au

Property Finance Made Simple

www.propertyfinancemadesimple.net.au

The Australian Property Investment Handbook 2018/19
www.Thehandbook.com.au

The 100K Property Plan
www.The100kpropertyplan.com.au

Children's books:
Billy and Harry love to play

Billy and Harry go to the zoo

Billy and Harry go to the beach

Billy and Harry go camping

Billy and Harry go on a winter holiday

Billy and Harry go to the playground

www.billyandharry.com.au

About the Author

Andrew Crossley lives in Melbourne, and is the #1 bestselling and award-winning author of three books: *Property Investing Made Simple, Property Finance Made Simple,* and *The Australian Property Investment Handbook 2018/19. The 100K Property Plan* is his fourth book in the *Made Simple* series. He has also written six children's books, entitled *Billy and Harry love to play.*

Andrew has worked in the finance and property industry for over twenty-two years, thirteen of those years in Australia. This included working for the largest non-bank and the largest mortgage manager in Australia during that time. He has also worked overseas in private wealth management on several continents.

Andrew is the founder of Australian Property Advisory Group (APAG), a buyer advocacy and property advisory business based in Melbourne, servicing all of Australia. APAG's buyer advocacy services specialise in working with investors, rather than people looking for a place to live, to reduce risk and improve potential with every investment property purchase. This is achieved through thorough research, leading to the shortlisting of 'where to buy,' sourcing of investment grade properties (the 'what to buy' to rent easily and remain in demand), and negotiation. APAG believes negotiating on a client's behalf will improve the chances of obtaining the property at a better price than what a client could do themselves, due to extensive negotiation and buying experience, often leading to a greater chance of saving the equivalent of the buyer's advocacy fee.

APAG offers tailor-made solutions and customised property investment plans to help investors, based on their current situation and their future goals, grow a portfolio which is well-balanced and affordable to maintain. Every person has a goal to retire comfortably and to have options available to them prior to retirement, whether to do volunteer work, travel more, or cut back on working hours. A tailored plan can provide a more achievable outcome than just buying an investment property and hoping for the best, or buying several properties without them being aligned to your circumstances and each other.

APAG was a finalist in the 2016 Australian Small Business Awards, highly recommended in the 2015 Investors Choice Awards in the categories of Property Investment Advisor and Buyer's Agent, and was national runner-up in the prestigious 2015 Readers' Choice Awards.

Property Industry Awards:

- *Finalist (Highly Recommended): Best Buyer's Agent in Australia, Readers' Choice Awards, 2016*

- *Runner Up: Best Buyer's Agent in Australia, Readers' Choice Awards, 2015*

- *Highly Recommended: Buyer's Agent, Investors Choice Awards, 2015*
- *Highly Recommended: Property Investment Advisor, Investors Choice Awards, 2015*

Finance Industry Awards:

- *NATIONAL WINNER: Australian Mortgage Awards (AMA), 2018*
- *NATIONAL WINNER: Mortgage and Finance Association of Australia (MFAA), 2017*
- *STATE WINNER: Mortgage and Finance Association of Australia (MFAA), 2017*
- *Finalist: Better Business Awards, 2017*
- *Finalist: Mortgage and Finance Association of Australia (MFAA), 2016*
- *Finalist: Mortgage and Finance Association of Australia (MFAA), 2015*
- *Finalist: Mortgage and Finance Association of Australia (MFAA), 2014*
- *Finalist: Australian Mortgage Awards, 2016*
- *Finalist: Australian Mortgage Awards, 2015*

Book Awards and Milestones:

Property Investing Made Simple

- *#1 Bestseller*

- *Best book: 'Real Estate' category, International Book Awards, 2015*
- *Best book: 'Real Estate' category, Book Excellence Awards, 2016*

Property Finance Made Simple

- *#1 Bestseller and #67 in all books on Amazon Kindle Australia*

The Australian Property Investment Handbook 2018/19

- *#1 Bestseller and #68 in all books on Amazon Kindle Australia*

Qualifications:

- *Accredited Property Investment Advisor, Property Investment Professionals of Australia (PIPA)*
- *Qualified Property Investment Advisor (QPIA)*
- *Fully licensed Real Estate Agent (NSW and VIC)*
- *Advanced Diploma in Financial Services (Financial Planning)*
- *Diploma in Finance (Mortgage Broking Management)*
- *Masters in Business Administration*
- *Masters in Commerce*
- *Masters in Commercial Law*

Andrew has also written for dozens of industry and non-industry publications, and has appeared on TV and radio. He is an educator, mentor, consultant, and public speaker.

Having grown a personal portfolio of over twelve properties, consisting of houses, townhouses, dual occupancies, and units across several states, Andrew was recognised in the *Your Investment Property Magazine* Property Investor of the Year Awards, 2012.

Personal Message:

I am sure you will enjoy reading my book as much as I have enjoyed writing it and sharing my knowledge and insights with you. Whether buying your first investment property or your next, it should be a worthwhile experience. To help ensure that it is an enjoyable experience, you need to arm yourself with the right information, then implement that information and use professionals in their fields to help you.

Blueprint

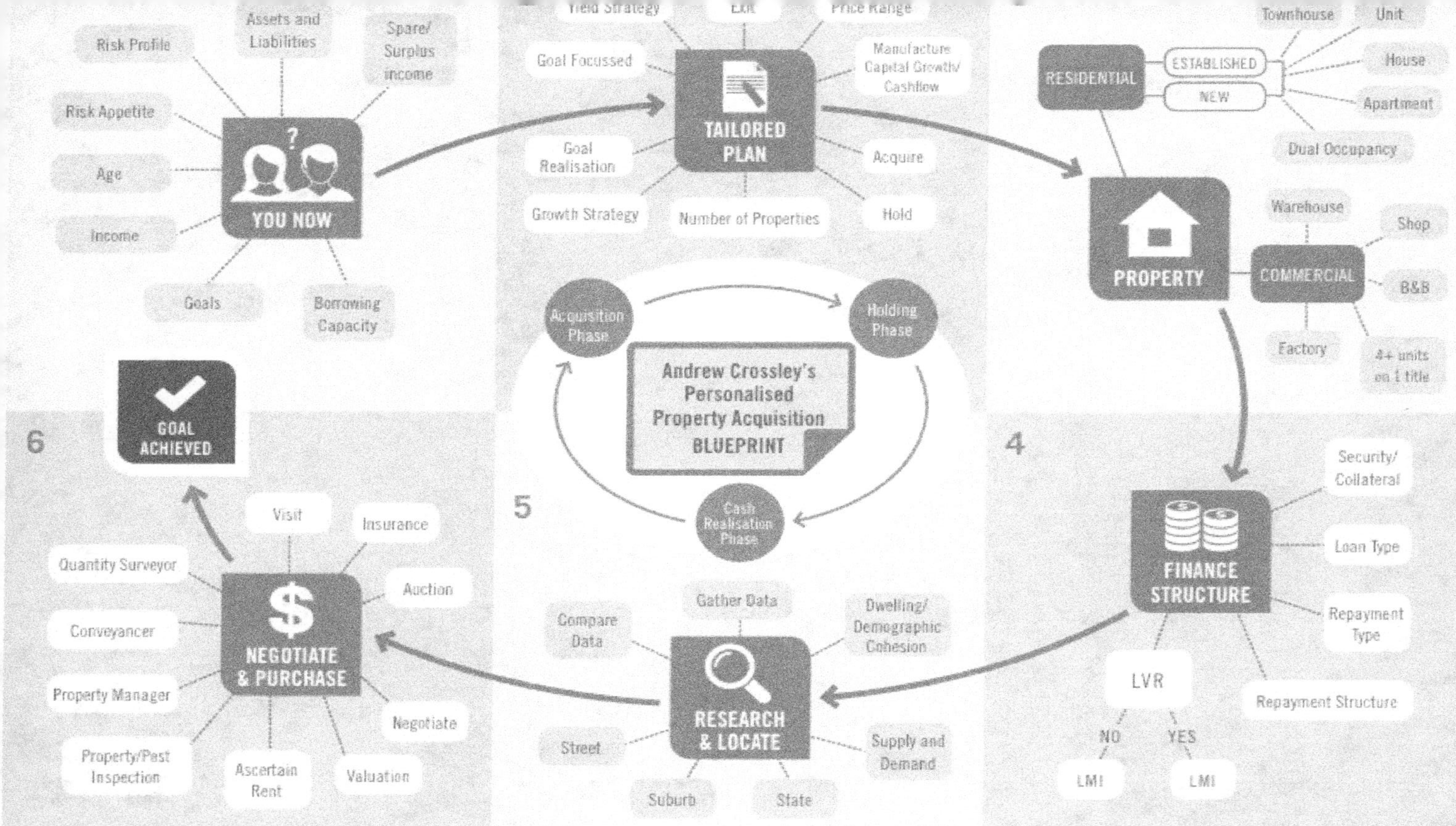
YOU NOW
Risk Profile
Assets and Liabilities
Spare/ Surplus income
Risk Appetite
Age
Income
Goals
Borrowing Capacity
TAILORED PLAN
Yield Strategy
Exit
Price Range
Goal Focussed
Manufacture Capital Growth/ Cashflow
Goal Realisation
Acquire
Growth Strategy
Number of Properties
Hold
PROPERTY
RESIDENTIAL
ESTABLISHED
NEW
Townhouse
Unit
House
Apartment
Dual Occupancy
COMMERCIAL
Warehouse
Shop
B&B
Factory
4+ units on 1 title
4
FINANCE STRUCTURE
Security/ Collateral
Loan Type
Repayment Type
Repayment Structure
LVR
NO
YES
LMI
LMI
5
Andrew Crossley's Personalised Property Acquisition BLUEPRINT
Acquisition Phase
Holding Phase
Cash Realisation Phase
RESEARCH & LOCATE
Gather Data
Compare Data
Dwelling/ Demographic Cohesion
Street
Supply and Demand
Suburb
State
6
NEGOTIATE & PURCHASE
GOAL ACHIEVED
Visit
Insurance
Quantity Surveyor
Auction
Conveyancer
Property Manager
Negotiate
Property/Pest Inspection
Ascertain Rent
Valuation

Chapter 1

Extending, Subdividing, Constructing, and Developing

Property development: scary, a piece of cake, or somewhere in between?

Your response will probably depend on whether you are a first-timer, a second-timer, or a veteran, and how much you know about the process. Of course, if you do have experience in property development, then your response will also be based on whether that experience was painless or painful.

Ultimately, for finance, the lender will require council approved plans and specifications, along with the fixed price building contract. It is a reasonable consideration that you do not sign a building contract unless it is a fixed price contract.

Having said that, most contracts will include a provisional sum to cover the builder for expenses that cannot reasonably be foreseen. An example of this could be discovering rock in the ground during the excavation process. Builders are then able to draw down on the provisional sum. Imagine $5000 is the provisional sum allowed. In the example just given, the removal of rock may cost $3000, and this would be invoiced to you. Unless another unforeseen scenario occurs, you would not need to pay the balance of $2000. It is important that you agree with the provisional sum included.

Subdividing and Strata

These are the two methods used to create new titles and more value in a property. Almost anyone can do this with the right sized block of land in the right area by applying to council to split the block. Subdividing one block may mean that you create two smaller land lots with individual titles, and you can then create smaller developments.

Bear in mind that a property does not necessarily have to be subdivided to build more than one dwelling on the land; you can strata the titles. Strata title refers to a situation where an individual or entity owns part of the property, such as the dwelling (e.g. townhouse, unit, or office), but they share ownership of the rest of the property, such as some or all of the land, driveways, gardens, foyers, or corridors in apartment buildings. Normally, more than two dwellings that share a driveway or common land require a body corporate/owner's corporation to be established to insure the land and manage the responsibility of the shared areas. Caravan parks, resorts, and retirement villages are more obvious examples of this. Strata titles are great for generating immediate value, as you can then sell separate parts of the property off. You may have heard the saying, "the sum of the parts are worth more than the whole."

You do not have to develop or build to gain value from applying to strata a title. A good friend of mine purchased several blocks of three or four units on a single title and successfully applied to council to strata the titles, creating an uplift in value of 200K.

Process

Be patient reading this; there are a number of considerations and processes. Remember, councils are obliged to follow specific timelines prescribed in the planning scheme. The statutory requirement is sixty days; however, the clock starts and stops at various intervals, primarily because councils require and request additional information. This may not suit your timeline, and could increase your costs (e.g. holding costs such as interest, or rent if you have to live elsewhere). However, the end result can be very rewarding and profitable, especially if you have been able to get the house you want by extending, rather than buying again and moving. You can save a lot in sale costs and taxes.

Let's start with a picture. A flowchart diagram is often easier than a written description. It is relevant for all types of projects. This example provides a snapshot of a good firm's process.

Be aware: many of the contents of this flowchart are not necessarily relevant to all states; there are some parts of the examples which will need to be changed if undertaking a project outside Victoria.

*refer to image on next page

And now comes some theory supporting the flowchart!

When it comes to property development, there are a lot of rules and regulations. As boring as they may seem, it is important to try to come to grips with them. You also need to understand some basic terms or definitions. Getting your head around these is critical to helping you along the way and with any future projects you may undertake.

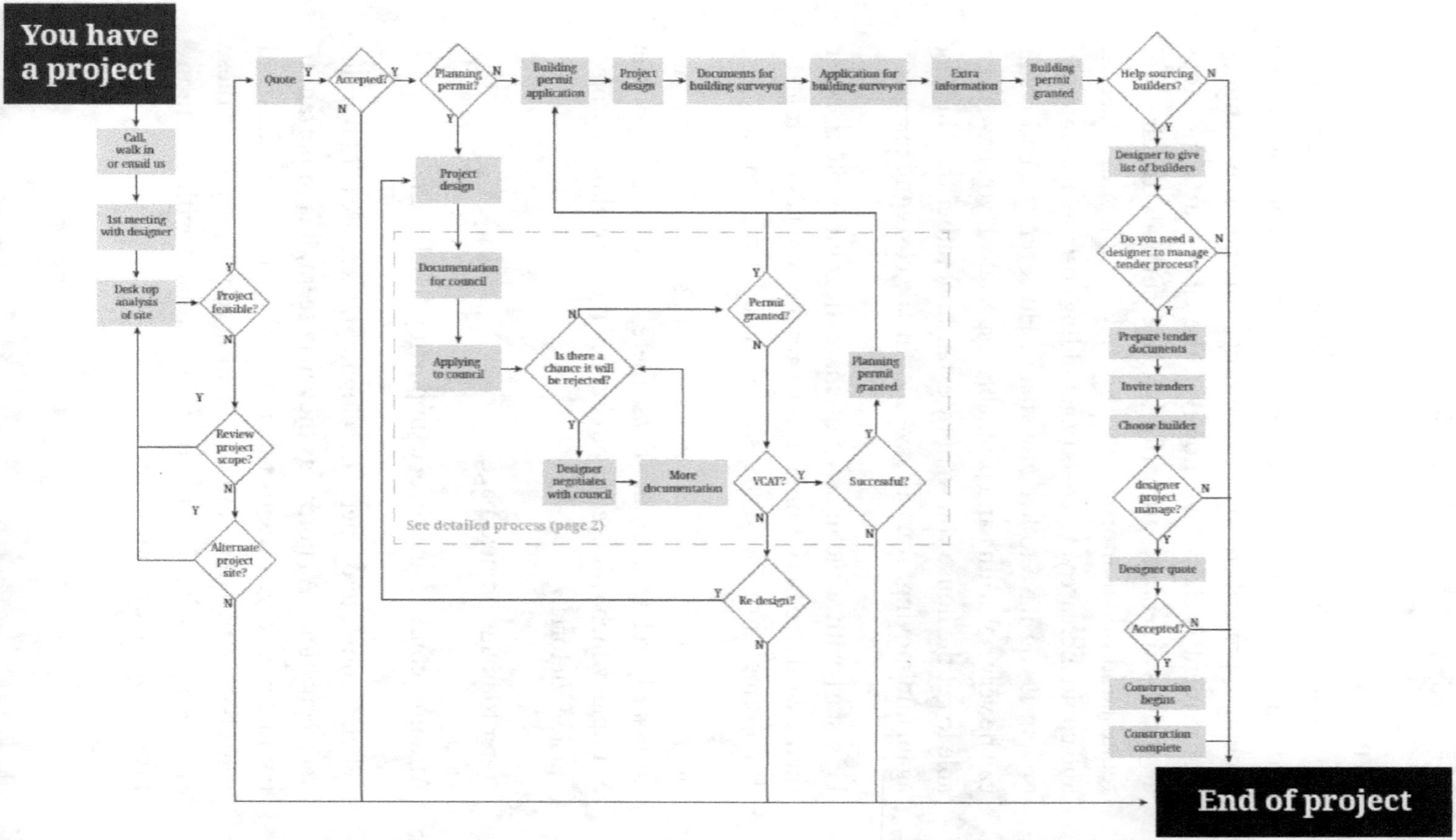

You have a project
Call, walk in or email us
1st meeting with designer
Desk top analysis of site
Project feasible?
Review project scope?
Alternate project site?
Quote
Accepted?
Planning permit?
Project design
Documentation for council
Applying to council
Is there a chance it will be rejected?
Designer negotiates with council
More documentation
Permit granted?
VCAT?
Successful?
Planning permit granted
Re-design?
See detailed process (page 2)
Building permit application
Project design
Documents for building surveyor
Application for building surveyor
Extra information
Building permit granted
Help sourcing builders?
Designer to give list of builders
Do you need a designer to manage tender process?
Prepare tender documents
Invite tenders
Choose builder
designer project manage?
Designer quote
Accepted?
Construction begins
Construction complete
End of project

Property development is not just about building a structure. It includes all activity that adds value to a piece of land or property, or changes how the land may be used (which can also be considered to add value).

Examples of property development include:

- *building a new home*
- *a renovation or extension obtaining a planning permit - which is permission to use the land in a certain way (e.g. creating units or townhouses)*
- *obtaining a building permit (permission to construct a project)*
- *'change of use' permits (e.g. turning a warehouse into a 24-hour gym or indoor trampoline center)*
- *the actual construction of projects.*

If you are a current or potential investor, let's get one thing sorted straight up: any investment carries risk, and that includes property development. There are absolutely no guarantees. But with research, planning, and experience, the level of risk can be minimised. So, let's get into the nitty gritty!

Councils have a document called a planning scheme, which incorporates their long-term vision and specifies how land will be used in their area (in keeping with their vision). You can, if you wish, read these on your local council website. This document will clarify whether you need a planning permit for your project. Sometimes the planning scheme is not as clear as you might hope, and it may be worthwhile having someone qualified and familiar with these types of matters to help you with interpretation. It can be complex, with lots of 'if this, then that.'

A planning permit is permission from your council to use or develop land in a certain way. There are allowable uses with a planning permit and allowable uses without a planning permit, as well as prohibited uses. A simple example is that you cannot have an industrial building/use of land in a residential area, or an extreme example is that a brothel will not be permitted in a residential area (thank goodness). Generally, a planning permit is required for units or commercial projects, but it may also be needed for some residential developments.

If a planning permit is required for your project, you will need to apply to the council for this. The application requires preliminary (conceptual) designs to be prepared and submitted, along with various plans and reports subject to the type of proposed development and the council involved (as they often differ in their requirements). The regulations are complex and it is wise to check before buying land.

A planning permit does not belong to a person or persons; it is issued *to* an applicant *for a particular property*. Often, properties are sold with a planning permit in place, and therefore a buyer can proceed with the development as specified by the permit and approved plans. They will then complete the next stage in applying for the building permit. It is very important to know that plans/permits for one property cannot be used on another property. You must obtain a separate permit for each one.

The process of applying for a planning permit is outlined on the next flowchart/diagram.

The Planning Permit Process

Prepare & submit the application to the Council of the area which includes plans, reports & documents (see Note 1)

→ Council responds advising receipt of the application and which Town Planner the application has been allocated to.

↓

The town planner makes a preliminary assessment (usually within 4 weeks) and may send a request for further information.

↓

If Council requests changes to the plans, these will be discussed with you / approved by you first. The amended plans will be resubmitted to Council (together with any additional information requested).

← If Council is satisfied with the above the application will progress to "Advertising". Letters will be sent to adjoining neighbours & a sign will be erected on the site (for two weeks) advising neighbours of the proposed development (or use). A fee is required, payable to Council to cover costs.

→ If council is satisfied that the application will not have negative impact or cause material detriment to any person the application will not be advertised.

↓

If advertising takes place, the sign is removed after the two week period and a statutory declaration is completed and returned to Council confirming the sign was displayed, during the advertising period.

↓

Council then assesses the application and in so doing:

- Considers any objections
- Holds a mediation meeting if needed
- Considers any comments/advice from other Council departments (eg engineering) or external agencies (eg Vicroads, Water Authorities)
- Assesses planning scheme provisions
- Negotiations with the permit application
- Prepares the report

↓

Council makes a decision about the application
Note: Council has 60 days in which to make its decision however please be aware that the "clock" starts & stops (See Note 2). If council takes longer than 60 days, we can apply for a review at VCAT*.

REFUSAL

If the application is refused, you have 60 days from the date of same to apply to VCAT* for a review of the decision.

Notice of Decision to Grant a Permit with Conditions
Despite any/some objections Council decides they will still issue a permit and objectors have 21 days to appeal the decision at VCAT*.

→ If an objector appeals, the application will be decided upon at the direction of VCAT* at a hearing.

↓

If there are no appeals within 21 days of the issue of the Notice of Decision to Grant a Permit, a Planning Permit is issued. (The conditions will also need to be addressed).

PERMIT with Conditions

We must address any/all of the Conditions on the Planning Permit and lodge amended plans as required which will be endorsed once approved by Council.

↓

If a permit condition is unacceptable we have 60 days from the date the permit (or notice of decision to grant a permit) is issued to apply for a review of the conditions with VCAT*.

↓

Conditions of the Permit will include the requirement for other plans (eg drainage and landscape which also need to be prepared & lodged with Council for approval).

NOTE 1 - Application Letter, Application Fee, Neighbourhood & Site Description Report, Design Response Report, Copy of Title less than 60 days old, Arborist Report (if needed), Photographs, Plans 3 x A1; 3 x A3, (Development plan, Elevations, Neighbourhood & Site, Design Response and Shadow Diagrams).

NOTE 2 - Eg. The "clock" stops during the advertising period, if Council requests further information or during mediation meetings.

*Victorian Civil and Administrative Tribunal.

A building permit, now more commonly issued by a private building surveyor (but still issued by some councils), is permission to build the proposed development.

The application requires preparation of construction plans (or working drawings) and the relevant documentation for the design. These are the plans a builder will work from during the construction of your project.

If a planning permit is required for the project, then the plans for the building permit application are required to match the concept designs/drawings approved for the planning permit.

A registered building practitioner is required to complete the plans and documentation for both planning and building permit applications.

The Land

If you already have your land, the first item to check off is your Certificate of Title. This will not only give you the dimensions of the site, but it will also detail any restrictions imposed upon the site. Some of the restrictions include:

Easements

An easement is a section of land registered on your property title where you cannot build, as there may be drains, for example. It gives someone the right to use the land for a specific purpose, even if they are not the landowners. Permission can be granted to build eaves over the easement, but this should not be taken as a given.

Covenants

Covenants were placed on titles many years ago, usually at the time of the original subdivision, to create some certainty about the type(s) of development that would occur on the land within the original subdivision.

Many residential lots have titles which contain restrictive covenants. Covenants can limit the use and development of land in various ways and therefore *may* cause some difficulties if the landowner wishes to develop their land.

The most common restrictions of covenants are as follows:

- *No more than one dwelling house and associated out-building may be erected.*
- *Only single-storey dwellings may be erected.*
- *Construction of a dwelling must be done with brick or any other approved (specified) material.*
- *The roof of any buildings must be slate or tiles (as opposed to metal deck).*
- *The value of the dwelling must not be less than a specified amount.*
- *No sand or earth may be removed from the land, or no quarrying on the land.*

Covenants can, in some cases, be removed when applying for a planning permit. As part of this process, or with the assistance of a solicitor, covenants may be removed by making an application through the courts.

Section 173 Agreements

This is an agreement reached under the named section of the Planning and Environment Act 1987 and is usually made with the council (the responsible authority) and the owner or potential purchaser of the land. The agreement will detail various conditions and/or restrictions about how the land can be developed or used, which can be registered on the title as well.

If you are on the hunt for just the right block, then request the sale documents, specifically the Section 32 Statement or equivalent in the relevant state. This is a statement by the owner/seller to potential purchasers and it details certain information about the property title that should be known before signing a contract to buy the land.

The information noted above (re: easements, covenants, and Section 173 agreements) can form part of your research so that you do not end up purchasing property that you cannot use as you would like.

You may like to consider employing the services of a buyer's agent, who can source land specific to your project, or approach someone or a business with specific knowledge and experience in planning and design prior to purchase/signing contracts.

The next step is to check the zoning for your land. This is part of the planning scheme mentioned earlier. Land is earmarked or zoned by councils to be used in a certain way, such as housing (residential), business, or industrial. For example, there are currently forty-eight zones in Victoria. Each one will have its own set of requirements and – dare I say it – restrictions. It will also specify whether a planning permit is needed, and the information that has to be provided and submitted to council with an application for a planning permit.

Overlays should also be considered. Overlays are a special feature of the land; examples include significant vegetation, heritage, or flood risks. As another example, there are also twenty-six different types of overlays in Victoria. You can find out how your land is zoned and if any overlays apply in a number of ways including:

- *contacting your local council*
- *checking the Section 32 Statement/equivalent*
- *contacting a consultant.*

Designing Your 'For Now' Home, Your Dream Home, or Maximising the Return on Your Investment?

This can be nerve-wracking because there is, without a doubt, a lot of money involved. So, it is important to be realistic. With *careful* planning, you can keep expenses to a minimum. There are lots of things to think about, and I will try to cover them all here.

Decisions, decisions! You could choose a spec home builder, a design and construct company, or a company that prepares custom designs. There are advantages and disadvantages to each option.

Spec Home Builder

Traditionally, this term means a new house is designed and constructed (display home), speculating that sales of that design will generate from an inspection. That is, you can purchase this house design for the company's fixed price on your land (but remember, conditions apply). Because of the volume build, the builder may receive bulk buying discounts, and could pass some of those discounts on to the purchaser.

Disadvantages include that the design may not suit your site, or take into account orientation to the sun, views, or neighbours. It is less likely to be in keeping with the character of the neighbourhood, and most likely unsuitable for land with fall (slope). As the term 'volume build' implies, there may be a number of similar dwellings in an area, thereby reducing resale value.

Design and Construct Company

This is where a building company quotes to build, renovate, or extend your home, and they include the design process as part of the package. It is a good way of knowing what the final costs are from the beginning, and some companies use in-house building designers to complete the design work.

Advantages include that these projects are designed specifically for your site and needs. The total cost includes the design process, and saves you the time and trouble of finding a builder and going to tender.

Disadvantages include that the projects are designed for profitability rather than an inspirational and functional design. You are unable to have this type of company design your project and then choose another builder. Furthermore, not every style of home is suitable for this kind of service. For example, some companies will only complete second-storey additions to certain types of homes.

A Custom Designed Home or Renovation

This is where you engage a company that specialises in creating personalised custom designs, such as a building designer. They will consult you regarding the land (pre-purchase if you require), your wish list for your home or renovation, and the regulations. They will create a design to marry your goals, the site's potential, and council regulations.

Advantages often include obtaining a better result, in that you have a custom design home or renovation tailored to meet your individual needs. Your design choices are only limited by site or council restrictions. The property will be designed to take advantage of the sun, any views, and to enhance the privacy and enjoyment of your home. Further, resale value is generally higher for custom designed homes.

The biggest disadvantage is that this option is more expensive than the other two. Most will say this downside is outweighed by the advantage of a personalised, custom design that suits your lifestyle or investment goals.

The custom design process will take into account:

- *your budget*
- *your family (existing/planned)*
- *lifestyle*
- *the land, including all the items noted earlier, such as the easements and other restrictions*
- *trees; there may be trees on the site that can be retained, or some may need to be removed. In some*

areas, permits are required to remove any trees, and this should be thoroughly investigated before tree removal is commenced.

- *there may be a building envelope, which means you can only build within that area on the site*
- *the type of property you're looking for (e.g. modern, period style, or open-plan living).*

So, What's The Important Stuff to Think About When Designing a New Dwelling?

Whilst there is no crystal ball, there are quite a few things that warrant attention and can produce better results:

- *think about how long you may live in the property, or what your goal is with the property (e.g. buy and hold, flip, or renting it out and living in it later).*
- *it should have owner-occupier appeal.*
- *corridors take up lots of room, so it could be worth trying to keep them to a minimum.*
- *think ahead - children become teenagers, and then adults, quickly. They need and want their own space(s), such as study areas. If you can afford it, there are a lot of advantages for adding ensuites (albeit smaller ones) off of their rooms; this would appeal to a wider demographic, and perhaps have better resale value.*
- *if the home you are planning is two-storey, think*

about cavity and storage spaces under the stairs, as well as sitting/storage areas at the landings.

- *if the budget is tight, you may also like to consider designing a bigger home, completing the 'shell' (exterior walls), and fitting out some of it later on (rather than doing an extension, which can be even more costly). Again, it depends on the purpose.*

- *consider the orientation of the home on the land (e.g. outdoor living areas facing north for passive solar energy and warmth).*

- *the connection between your indoor and outdoor living areas should flow.*

- *street appeal; I hear of so many people who love living in their property, whether it is their own or a rental, but dislike the first impression of the house.*

- *location of windows and the furniture you already have*

- *the design will need to take into account any slope on the land and any other natural features.*

This list can seem quite extensive, but a great designer should challenge you to think of all of the above, and then some!

Once you have finalised your design and sketch plans have been completed to a sufficient level of detail, a preliminary costing can be prepared by either a quantity surveyor (QS), building cost estimator, or a builder. This will give you a gauge of how much it will cost to build. This could be an important step before proceeding with the construction (working drawings), because it is easier to change the design at this point if the indicative build cost comes in too high. If you wait until the construction drawings are complete or the building permit has been issued, changes after this point will incur additional design/documentation fees (most likely for the building surveyor to amend the permit).

It is well worth discussing your overall budget with the designer, as this can impact significantly upon the designer's approach and suggestions that will be made to you. For example:

Affordability Budget

– making the best use of the limited funds available. This requires a design that achieves excellent value for money.

Staged Budget

– the entire budget is not available in one lump sum, but may be available over time in a couple of or multiple instalments. The designer would create the overall design of the build that could be completed in stages. Generally, planning permits and building permits are valid for two years (you can also apply for extensions, although this should not be relied upon).

Development Budget

– the primary goal is to obtain a profit on the sale of the property within a couple of years.

Capitalisation Conscious Budget

– the owner and designer are trying to reduce the risk of overcapitalisation on the property. Overcapitalisation may occur if the money spent on the home is likely to be greater than the potential resale value. A number of factors come into play when assessing the risk of overcapitalisation, such as location, quality of the work, size of the home (or renovation), and the state of the market at the time.

On another note, some believe that quality of life and lifestyle is more important in the family home than the risk of overcapitalising. If this is an investment property, you should not have your owner-occupier hat on, but you should have your commercial hat on. Yes, the property should have appeal, but many things have appeal with less expensive inclusions.

Investment Budget

– the aim is to achieve long-term rents from the investment property (and, quite likely, capital growth and low maintenance costs).

The cost of building your home (or renovation/extension) can vary considerably based upon:

- *whether you are renovating or building new (the former is often more expensive per square metre)*
- *the size of the project*
- *the type of construction (e.g. the type of roof or exterior cladding)*
- *the number of areas requiring fittings and fixtures, such as bathrooms, ensuites, kitchens, and laundries, as well as the quality of the fittings and fixtures*
- *the slope of the site – the steeper the site, the more it usually costs to build on. Because foundations and supporting structures are different, additional*

excavation may be needed, along with the addition of retaining walls, for example.

- *access to the site for the delivery and handling of materials*
- *the type of soil conditions on the site, which may impact upon the foundations needed*
- *whether rock is present on the site, potentially requiring additional excavation*
- *availability of services, such as water supply, storm water, sewer lines, electricity, gas, and phone*
- *a contingency sum: an amount usually allowed by most builders to cover unforeseen costs. For example, undertaking a renovation/extension has been known to lead to the discovery of termites in the frame, which then requires replacement and treatment for further protection. A contingency sum could usually be around 5–10% of the budget.*
- *accurate and complete documents, which will minimise delays in the planning and building process.*

Developing your Backyard (more traditionally known as 'Dual-Occupancy')

If two or more dwellings are proposed for a block of land, a planning permit is required.

It is absolutely essential that you have a designer who can determine if your project is feasible. Feasibility means that, based upon the designer's knowledge of the council planning scheme, the zone for the land, their understanding of any restrictions, and council's preferred developments for the area, you are more likely to achieve a permit than not. And if it *is* feasible, what exactly does that mean? There is no 100% guarantee that your project will receive a planning permit (or permission from council).

When a planning permit is required, the following information needs to be gathered and prepared:

1. Planning Permit Application Form

Complete the application form for a planning permit and pay the relevant application fee.

2. Copy of Title

A clear, legible copy of the certificate of title, showing current ownership of the land, needs to be provided and submitted with the application when it is lodged with council. The copy of title must be current and could range from one month to three months old (depending on the relevant council). Details of any registered covenants/restrictions on the land must also be provided.

3. Reports

These reports detail the proposal's consistency with the objectives of the State Planning Framework, Local Planning Policy Framework, and the Municipal Strategic Statement.

4. Site Re-Establishment and Feature Surveys

These surveys are prepared by a licensed land surveyor and provide information about the site, such as levels, contours, and the position of fences and trees. You may contact a surveyor of your choice, or your designer may be able to arrange an external consultant on your behalf.

5. Neighbourhood and Site Description Plan and the Design Response Plan

These plans detail all properties within a fifty-metre radius (at a minimum) of the subject site, and address all of the requirements of the relevant clauses of the local council's planning scheme, as well as how the proposed development responds to the neighbourhood.

6. Photographs

Detailed photographs of the subject site and surrounding properties (including those opposite the site) are required to be submitted with the application.

7. Site/Floor Plan

The site/floor plan is required to include the following:

- *the dimensions of the land as detailed on the certificate of title*
- *a floor plan, with description indicating the use of all rooms*
- *the location and internal dimensions of any garages, car spaces, and/or carport structures*
- *setbacks from all boundaries*
- *adjoining building envelopes/windows facing the subject site within nine metres of the property boundaries*

- *location and width of existing and/or proposed vehicle crossovers (driveways)*
- *location, height, and the construction materials of existing and/or proposed fencing*
- *site levels and finished floor levels to the Australian Height Datum (AHD)*
- *any existing vegetation proposed to be retained – with details including height and full botanical name*
- *location and size of any easements on/or adjacent to the site.*

8. Elevations

Dwelling

The elevations must be provided for all sides (of all dwellings) and detail the following:

- *the natural ground level, and the height of the finished floor levels above the natural ground level*
- *external wall heights and overall building heights, measured from natural ground level*
- *the position of all windows, along with the sill height of the windows, measured from the finished floor level*
- *the location and extent of any proposed cut and fill.*

Front Fence

The elevations of the front fence are required to detail:

- *construction materials and finishes*
- *dimensions of all components of the fence, as measured above natural ground level.*

9. Shadow Diagrams

On separate plans, shadow diagrams must be supplied at the hours of 9.00 am, 12.00 noon, and 3.00 pm on the 22nd of September (this date is midway between the shortest and the longest days of the year).

10. Schedule of External Finishes, Materials, and Colours including:

- *All external walls*
- *Roof*
- *Fascia*
- *Window frames*
- *External doors*
- *Paving, including car park surfacing.*

11. Arborist Report

The Arborist Report should detail all established, significant trees on-site, or on adjoining land within five metres of the property boundary. The condition of the trees will be assessed including:

- *accurate location*
- *full botanical name*

- *DBH (diameter of trunk at breast height) – i.e. trunk caliper at approximately 1.4 metres above ground*
- *critical root zone*
- *health, structure, and form of the trees*
- *the tolerance of each tree to the proposed development works*
- *suitability for retention*
- *tree protection measures, if retained.*

12. Development Summary

The development summary will provide information for both existing and proposed conditions including:

- *site area*
- *number of dwellings*
- *floor areas*
- *number of car spaces*
- *area of private/total open space*
- *building site coverage*
- *percentage of impervious surfaces.*

13. Plans and Elevations

Copies of all plans and elevations will be required in either A3 or A4 size, in addition to A1 plans submitted with the application.

14. Additional Information

Additional information may be required if the land is subject to a Heritage Overlay, a Special Building Overlay, or any other overlay. An overlay, as I have previously touched on, is a council control. It could relate to, for example, tree/vegetation protection, siting, or specified size of subdivisions. Note: there may be more than one overlay that applies to an area.

15. Development Contributions

Some councils impose a development contribution fee, which is used for the establishment and/or maintenance of parks and council infrastructure.

16. Landscape Plan

This details areas of the site to be landscaped, as well as specifying the materials and plants that will be used for both the common and private areas of the proposed development.

Councils may differ slightly in their requirements for planning applications because they have their own Housing Strategy or municipal planning scheme. Examples of this include coastal, rural, and metropolitan. As these areas can differ greatly, it makes sense that their planning schemes would too.

It is difficult to determine how long it will take for a typical town planning application. This depends upon the size of the project and the council involved. Generally four to six months would need to be allowed. A quick turnaround has been completed in as little as forty-five days, while the longer side of things could stretch to two years, or if you are unlucky, even more.

Once a planning permit has been received, the next step in the process is obtaining a building permit. Refer back to the "You have a project" flowchart for an outline of the process. The building permit process is usually quite straightforward and does not take as long as a planning permit. Approximately four to six weeks should be allowed.

If a planning application is refused a permit, you could have the option to appeal at VCAT (Victorian Civil Administrative Tribunal) or your state equivalent. This is also detailed on the "Planning Permit Process" flowchart.

Renovations and Extensions

Hereafter, these projects will be affectionately called 'renos.' Let's be honest – they are not for the fainthearted!

They can be challenging at worst, and frustrating at best, but they can also be extremely rewarding if one thinks laterally, begins with the end in mind, has a bucketload of patience, and is willing to be flexible. And you might need to get used to a bit – ok, a lot – of dust as well. For some people, and subject to the size of the reno, you might like to factor accommodation into the budget!

Renos can be more expensive per square metre, so a realistic budget and a bit of cash (or a loan) will not go astray. Bear in mind that if you were to sell your home and buy elsewhere, the buying and selling costs alone can equate to $100,000. So, redirecting and putting this money into your current place of residence, or the house you have just purchased, can be very worthwhile.

The first message is to dig deep. Get real about your goals. Ask yourself what you are trying to achieve in doing the reno in the first instance?

Some might argue that you can never overcapitalise on your own home/lifestyle, but this does not mean making your house a mansion in the worst street or the worst suburb is the wisest choice. Having said that, if you are planning to stay for the long term, at least seven to ten years post-reno (which is the next property cycle period), then you will most likely see a return on your financial investment.

Unless you were the original designer of the home and know exactly what happened on-site during the construction process, you will not know what is behind the walls or under the roof until the various materials are removed in the demolition part of your renovation. This means your reno will be designed based on the current floorplan, and what is reasonable to assume is behind the walls and under the roof. This is irrespective of whether you have the original plans or not. If you do not have an original/current copy of the plans, a full measure up and re-draw of the existing house will need to be done.

It is important to know that sometimes builders and/or carpenters will make changes along the way during the construction process, as do homeowners. These changes may be to get a better result on-site. Once the plaster has been removed, and what is behind is revealed, the construction may need to be done differently to what was planned (e.g. how it was drawn on the plans).

The advantage of being on-site throughout the reno process is that decisions can be made on the spot if need be. In some instances, these changes may need to and/or should go back to council and/or a building surveyor for approval, but often they do not.

So, the plans are prepared, based on what can be seen at the time and what the homeowner wants. All structural work will require a building permit and most renos will be in this category. Some will require a planning permit too. For example, if your property has a foothills overlay or a bushfire management overlay, these will trigger the need for a planning permit.

The next section will feature a case study about a significant renovation (and, yes, extension).

Scenario

Client:

Mum, Dad, and three children (6, 9, and 12 years old respectively).

Project:

Second-storey addition to the house, and renovation/upgrade of other areas.

Specifics:

New master bedroom, ensuite, study, and retreat area.

Combine kitchen, existing study, family room, and part of existing deck into one, open plan area.

Design/fit out new kitchen.

Construct new deck.

Required removal of load bearing walls, and engineering computations for beams (to replace the load bearing walls). Additional footings were also required underneath the existing house.

Goal:

No one in the family wanted to move. The house was aging, and the parents had a desire for better living spaces for their growing family in the longer term (ten years or longer).

Constraints:

Slope of the land

An overlay on the site meant that the overall size of the house (and deck) could not exceed 40% site cover.

Permits:

The renovation required a planning permit and building permit.

This type of project is significant and involved quite a few thousand dollars. A builder was engaged, rather than the clients managing the project and all the tradespeople required themselves. This is completely recommended when you are not in the building industry or do not have experience in renovating a property.

The project commenced in February and took approximately six months to complete. The family only moved out for one week whilst the new flooring was laid/sealed.

Challenges:

Dust, dust, and more dust. This meant nightly sessions with the vacuum cleaner to reduce the dust and make living in the space as easy as possible.

At one point, a tradesperson's foot went through the ceiling (in an area not even being renovated)! One of the carpenters working on the new upper-storey frame accidentally stepped onto and through the ceiling below. The builder was required to patch and repair this (at his expense).

Managing the renovation and everyday life through winter – particularly with a makeshift kitchen and huge tarpaulin(s) on the roof for an extended period of time. To begin with, the tradies were able to complete a fair proportion of the renovation without coming inside. However, an upper-storey renovation requires removal of a portion of the existing roof at some point. A tarpaulin was then placed over the makeshift roof, which is often not watertight nor wind resistant.

Some of the local wildlife invited themselves inside (eeek!) – because of the tarpaulin roof, there were many nooks making this possible. The family would hear the rustling of said wildlife in the night and have to evict them.

Another challenge was looking after the family pets and making sure they did not escape with so many people coming and going was also a challenge at times.

The "TARDIS" (a.k.a. the builders loo) at the front of the property was a bit of an eyesore.

Their front lawn was, essentially, murdered, and some of their plants suffered the same fate.

A final challenge was cleaning up after tradespeople, as each person's definition of clean can be completely different! As mentioned earlier, the vacuum cleaner worked overtime and ultimately had to be replaced!

Outcome:

The final product was an updated and much more modern, appealing home. It contained fabulous new living spaces, with separate areas for study and quiet times. As a result, family members no longer had the feeling that they were 'on top of one another.'

There were no budget blowouts as considerable thought had gone into the design (which is always a good thing).

Would They Have Done Anything Differently?

The family only wished that they had done the renovation/extension years earlier so that they could have had more time to enjoy the new areas. It was the best thing they ever did.

Renos can be a daunting, confronting, and messy exercise, but with appropriate planning and guidance, a fabulous result can be achieved. Try not to be swayed by horror stories; often these are the result of trying to cut corners and/or doing the project on the smell of an oily rag. Be guided by the experts, and what you really want and need for you and your family!

In Summary

Extending, subdividing, constructing, and developing are not projects to be undertaken by those who are time poor! They are projects that are potentially, or most likely, better suited to those who wish to buy and hold, or buy and flip.

Mistakes often made by owner builders are using credit cards to pay for works, allowing emotion in the decision making process (regarding any upgrades and inclusions), not allowing a buffer, and/or fully assessing feasibility.

With many, if not all, of these projects, they can carry slightly higher risk (which is variable, based upon who undertakes them) in that more time and expertise is usually needed. However, the results can be positive with higher yield, more growth and profit potential, and, therefore, increased wealth.

It is important to understand all the financial aspects involved, which include cost, risk, time, effort versus reward, sell versus hold, and also making allowances for profits (around 20%). Tax and time can dilute the return on investment, plus one should consider opportunity costs.

Note: Listen to my interview on Sky News about renovations via this link below:

https://twitter.com/SkyNewsRE/status/842933786044059648

Chapter 2

Commercial Finance and Property

In Australia, more than half of Australia's workforce are employed by over two million small to medium enterprises:

ABS – http://www.abs.gov.au/ausstats/abs@.nsf/mf/8165.0,
ASIC – https://asic.gov.au/for-business/your-business/small-business/small-business-overview/,
ASBFEO – https://www.asbfeo.gov.au/sites/default/files/Small_Business_Statistical_Report-Final.pdf. The commercial industry is growing rapidly, and exceeds 400 billion.

Industrial, office space, and retail properties make up the commercial landscape. Demographic patterns will influence some commercial sectors. Infrastructure for healthcare and aged care is becoming the norm in holiday destinations, with baby boomers seeking out a sea change. The growing demand for childcare services has created a need for this type of commercial property, while the rise of online shopping has created a larger demand for warehouses.

Our growing population has put pressure on the availability and cost of parking in capital cities; investing in a single or commercial car park is becoming popular.

The biggest difference with this market and the residential market is that it is more macro and Government policy conditions affect the commercial space. Economics, as distinct from market conditions, can vary across commercial property grades and regions and due to consumer spending on the back of interest rates and the economy. This, in turn, influences the success of the tenant occupying your property and their ability to stay in business, which will all impact on your property. Commercial property is riskier when it comes to vacancy. More macro level classifications apply to commercial property; entire sectors can be affected at any one time within an entire region, rather than being more centric to a particular suburb. Tourist accommodation, retail property, offices, and industrial spaces can all suffer across an entire region.

According to the ANZ/Property Council Survey 2018, capital growth in recent years has been supported by foreign investment. Population growth does support the retail sector, but if the Australian dollar starts rising, it can negatively impact tourism. On the whole, it is investors looking for yield that support the demand for commercial property. The problem with commercial property is its inherent lack of long-term, stable growth – just like the stock market, which is directly linked to the corporate world.

Many experts say that there is a high percentage of business failure in the first two years. 60% of small businesses fail in the first three years, according to *Inside Small Business* (Source: https://insidesmallbusiness.com.au/planning-management/why-most-small-businesses-fail-within-the-first-three-years). Vacancy rates can be high, which soon offset the higher yields of around 8%.

Commercial property may include a business, shop, retail, resort-style offices, factories, farms, multi-unit developments, warehouses, industrial units, mixed residential and commercial use, and income-producing properties. The list goes on. The value of the properties concerned are based on the rental returns. Often, the tenant pays all the outgoings (e.g. insurance, rates, and fit out). This is a separate market to residential, which requires different knowledge and due diligence. This type of property can possibly be good for diversifying your portfolio, given it can typically have higher yields.

Strata offices are becoming popular, as tenants can rent them close to where they live; this allows them to escape the distractions and interruptions at home, and expand their business at the same time. Remember, strata title refers to a situation where an individual/entity owns part of the property, such as the dwelling (e.g. townhouse, unit, or office), but they share ownership of the rest of the property.

Standard residential and commercial lenders will generally only lend up to 75% as a maximum, and can lend up to and over $2.5 million for a commercial investment property. Whilst fifteen-year terms are more common, thirty years is also possible. Lenders have dedicated lending teams for commercial property, due to the bespoke nature of the industry and the diversity in economic conditions that may come to bear on a credit decision. The biggest difference with commercial finance is that it does not fall into a predefined set of boxes as easily as residential lending does, because it is less predictable. The type of documentation required is similar to a residential loan, whether low documentation or full documentation. However, with commercial lending, future cash flow forecasts can be considered, rather than the black and white approach of residential lending. Commercial lending is normally a non-coded loan.

Repayment frequency can be the same as residential lending (weekly, fortnightly, or monthly) with additional repayments allowed on fixed rates, though monthly repayments are normally used. There are sometimes early termination fees attached to the loan. Some lenders do provide unlimited cash out to 75% LVR (Loan to Value Ratio), and this can also be used for working capital and purchase of business equipment.

Trading businesses are more popular with lenders, providing a product or service as distinct from property sales activities, as these are less impacted (generally speaking) by the property industry as an economy. Non-developer businesses are more nimble, while, for example, a developer would find it problematic to reduce a thirty-unit development down to fifteen.

Brokers are even more important in commercial finance; they can add significant value in packaging a deal up and selling it to the funder. Policy is less straightforward with commercial finance. Factors such as inventory finance, asset finance, unsecured finance, cash flow, and equipment and car finance must all be factored in (these financial details are beyond the scope of this book).

Commercial finance is the offering of loans for business purposes. The lender will need to be satisfied as to the business purpose, and any such lending is not covered under the National Consumer Credit Protection Act 2009.

A few examples of commercial finance include the purchase of a motor vehicle that is used predominantly for business use, commercial property (by nature and/or use), and business overdrafts and trade facilities (such as letters of credit, cash flow funding, or simply a loan to set up or purchase a business). However, for the purpose of this chapter, we will focus primarily on finance for commercial property.

The Upside of Commercial Property

Purchasing a commercial property for investment purposes is a genuine alternative to investing in residential property. One of the main benefits of owning commercial property against residential property is that the tenant generally covers all outgoings (property ownership costs), which are paid in addition to the rent. This means that the tenant pays for the rates, insurance, body corporate, and any other property ownership costs (other than land tax) which apply to the commercial property. Furthermore, the cost of preparing a commercial lease may also be the responsibility of the tenant. This generally results in a much higher yield to the owner.

Another benefit of commercial property is that the tenant may update and improve the property in order to make it better suit their business needs (e.g. fitting out the property for use is generally at the tenant's cost). Any modifications to the property may also require the tenant to 'make good' the property at the end of the lease. Tenants will generally maintain the property in top condition, as it is important to their business image, staff, and customers. Compare this to a residential investment; the landlord of a residential property has to ensure the property is presented at its best in order to attract a tenant, and the costs of any improvements are generally at the hand of the landlord.

Commercial properties also tend to have longer lease terms,

which offer the landlord a greater degree of comfort and ability to forecast cash flow. Leases normally have annual reviews, often last more than three years, and may also include options for further terms.

The Downside of Commercial Property

On the downside, commercial property may be more sensitive to the state of the economy, and values can be greatly affected at times of economic downturns. A commercial property may remain untenanted for a longer period as businesses seek to reduce costs or downsize when the economy slows down. Furthermore, commercial properties tend to lag behind residential properties when it comes to capital growth during economic upturns. Values are very much aligned to the performance of the economy and business sentiment. As for residential property, we all need a roof over our heads, whether we choose to rent or purchase an owner-occupied property. Therefore residential property is less aligned to the performance of the economy, and more aligned to supply and demand factors, which are directly impacted by population growth and the number of new dwellings being constructed.

Commercial property supply and demand can be influenced by a range of factors including changes in infrastructure, local supply levels, specific requirements of potential business tenants, and business sentiment. Importantly, the value of a commercial property is largely influenced by the quality of tenant and lease term, so there is a higher level of expertise required when considering the investment value equation.

Financing Commercial Property

Corelogic, in June 2018, determined that there were just under 20,000 commercial real estate transactions, with an estimated $15.2 billion spent on industrial property alone (Source: Corelogic - https://www.corelogic.com.au/news/rise-industrial-real-estate-2018). Commercial properties can take many shapes and forms. A lender will look at the property to establish its business purpose, and will also take into consideration a number of other variables including the property's zoning, any existing permits, current and future use, and the income-producing nature of the property. Examples of commercial properties include offices, car parks, warehouses, retail shops, farming land, hotels and pubs, petrol stations, and properties with specialised use (e.g. aged care and hospitals). Residential property development (as a general rule, greater than four dwellings on one title) can also qualify under commercial lending, as such residential property development establishes an intention to generate profit. As a result of its large range of uses, commercial property finance carries many more complexities compared to residential property lending. Each application is often reviewed on a case-by-case basis, with the lender able to take a more flexible approach to lending criteria. There can be a significant difference in lending criteria from one lender to another.

Before you seek commercial finance from a lender, you should prepare a business plan and cash flow forecast. These two reports will assist the lender's credit assessment of your application. The quality of your submission could potentially impact on the final interest rate the lender attributes to your loan. It would be a good idea to involve your lawyer to review potentially complex commercial lease agreements, and your accountant for financial advice and preparation of cash flow forecasts. Also seek the services of a finance broker with strong commercial lending experience.

Unlike residential property loans, which can have a loan term of up to thirty years, commercial property loans generally provide for a maximum loan term of fifteen years. Lenders will sometimes consider providing you with an interest-only period (although you will generally be asked to justify this request), and you will have to take into consideration the cash flow impact of paying principal and interest repayments over a shorter loan term.

As a rule, you will need to have a larger upfront deposit contribution when purchasing commercial property. This requirement varies from lender to lender, and you will find that most lenders will only lend between 65–80% of the commercial property valuation (this percentage is the LVR). The overall LVR can be influenced by a number of factors, including bank policy, strength of the applicant, security risk as outlined in the valuation report, quality of tenant and lease, and term of loan sought.

There is no mortgage insurance applicable for commercial property finance, however lender fees and charges are generally much higher compared to residential property finance. You should expect to pay a higher interest rate compared to a residential home loan. You will often have to cover upfront costs, including a lender establishment fee, a risk fee, bank valuation fee, legal documentation fee, and most loan accounts also come with monthly or quarterly account maintenance fees. Most lenders will negotiate pricing, however, the stronger the application and risk mitigants, the better chances of achieving a lower overall pricing outcome. The interest rate offered by a lender will be influenced by an assessed risk margin, which the lender calculates after considering the credit strengths and weaknesses specific to your application. You should also factor in any monthly, quarterly, or annual bank fees when calculating the effective interest rate.

There are some lenders who mainly concentrate on residential loans, but wish to have exposure to the commercial property market. These lenders often have more simplified commercial loan products (which are highly competitive) and lender criteria, and they offer what is referred to as a 'pure asset lend' against established commercial properties. These types of loans are very similar to your standard home loan in that the product is a 'set and forget' type of loan. The lender does not implement any financial covenants on your loan that sometimes require the borrower to provide annual financial statements for review and/or maintain the LVR at a minimum level (therefore avoiding any potential future lender's request for revaluation of your property in the future).

When considering commercial property for rental purposes, some lenders may offer a 'lease doc' product. This type of loan criteria essentially relies upon the rental income from a commercial lease to service the loan. These types of commercial loan products are niche products. Gross rental income of 1.5 multiplied by interest cover (150% of the interest repayment amount) is a good guide when seeking a lease doc commercial product. Furthermore, the quality of tenant may also influence credit decisioning. For example, a large corporation as a tenant would be looked on more favourably than a start-up business.

When considering a commercial loan agreement, you should

pay particular attention to any financial covenants outlined in the loan contract. A financial covenant is a requirement on the borrower to ensure that, during the term of the loan, you are able to demonstrate compliance with the requirement(s) stated in your loan contract. As mentioned above, financial covenants may include minimum net profit (EBITDA – Earning before interest, tax, depreciation and amortisation), minimum LVR, and reference to annual turnover. If you fail to meet the financial covenants outlined in your loan contract, you may be required to pay down your loan or even repay the whole debt, which could put you under significant financial stress. Making the loan repayments on time and with perfect conduct does not mean you can abandon your financial covenants. Sometimes you may be better off securing a loan that has a higher annual interest cost with no financial covenants, rather than securing a lower annual interest cost loan with strict financial covenants.

When seeking a commercial loan for property, you should engage the services of a finance broker as the range of products and lender credit criteria, as well as the subjective assessment nature of commercial lending, may be overwhelming.

Deposit Requirements

The LVR is more conservative under commercial property lending as the financial risk factors are generally exposed to a greater number of variables. There is no 'one size fits all' solution when it comes to commercial finance. Each application is assessed on a case by case basis.

The four major Australian banks have traditionally had a stronghold on commercial finance, however we are beginning to see a number of second-tier and specialist lenders entering this space who are often able to provide a more simplified approach to financing. An example of a simplified approach is a lease doc loan product. The lender is generally looking at the quality of tenant and the strength of a lease. Often a lender will require an existing lease to be in effect for a minimum of twelve months. Lease doc products are generally short-term (one to five years long), and generally align with the remaining term of the lease in place.

Low Documentation Loans

Since the global financial crisis of 2007/2008, the finance sector has made significant changes in the way they assess the borrower and the types of products offered. One of the main products which has lost support of the lenders is the low documentation loan.

Low documentation loans are loans where the lender is provided with supporting income documents that are less rigorous in nature, and the applicant must be self-employed. The income put forward for servicing the loan is by and large self-declared by the borrower and backed up by a range of income documents, including the most recent ATO Business Activity Statement(s), trading account statements, and accountant-signed declarations. These types of commercial loans are geared for the Small to Medium Enterprise (SME) business owners and offer an alternative solution to the mainstream lending channel. Low documentation loans by and large require brick and mortar backed securities, and the LVRs are commonly under 75%.

We have seen a gradual winding down of these types of loan products in the mainstream marketplace, with lenders stepping up the minimum document requirements. Whilst commercial borrowers receive a lower level of protection from the Government, commercial borrowers are still protected against unconscionable conduct and misleading and deceptive conduct. Low documentation loans still have a place in the market and are a viable alternative to full documentation loans.

Should you Lease or Buy a Premises?

This is an ongoing dilemma for many businesses. When a business commences operation, it is important to concentrate on cash flow and establishing the business. It is probably wise to not outlay unnecessary capital until the business is established. Over time, the choice may be out of the owner's hands as growth and the need for more size, among many other factors, may lead to the decision being made for the owner.

There are a number of considerations, drawbacks, and benefits when deciding whether to lease or buy a business premises. The starting point (besides the considerations detailed below) could be to seek advice from an accountant to model the costs of purchasing a premises and compare this to leasing costs.

The fundamental needs of the business must be assessed first.

Considerations

Floor space: the cost per square metre can impact on the affordability of purchasing the premises; it may be more cost effective to lease the space. Licenses, permits, and allowable use need to be factored in.

Visibility: Better placed premises in a suburb can cost more to purchase than to lease, in which case leasing may be better.

Signage: This is important for many service and product businesses alike.

Parking: It is very important to have parking available for clients. Clients are required to come to the business, rather than the business coming to them. Restaurants, cafés, and hotels (to name a few) list access (parking and wheelchair/disabled access) near the top of their priority list. Access, with a consideration of anti-discrimination laws, is important.

Location: With the internet, location is becoming less important. The suitability of the environment and the demographic of the business' clients can lead to the decision being made for the owner, depending on affordability, so that they can be situated in an appropriate location. Proximity of suppliers, distributors, and clients, as well as complimentary services offered by other businesses, all play their role

Budget: The bottom line; having the borrowing capacity, the deposit, and the ability to borrow based on tax returns or income will ultimately determine the choices that a business has.

Purchasing a separate commercial property is a matter of comparing the cost to rent your own premises versus the cost of having a mortgage against an owned property. Consider the location, the opportunity cost with respect to whether there is a better location you could purchase a commercial property in for investment, and whether rental income from another premises could earn you or save you more money than purchasing your own premises (and the growth on the property in its location).

Benefits of Owning a Commercial Property

Owning an asset, which can grow to provide a nest egg, is the most obvious benefit. Wealth, therefore, can be increased on two fronts rather than just one. The first one being goodwill (reputation and client base), and the next being a tangible, growing in value asset. The growing equity in the property is effectively, in itself, a separate business. This can then be accessed to provide the capital for expansion, working capital, and weathering any storm that may come the business' way.

Fitting out a leased premises to operate a business can be easier than fitting out a leased residential dwelling, particularly from a permission from the landlord perspective, but it does provide more freedom to own the premises. A financial planner can advise if it is considered appropriate to purchase the premises with a self-managed superfund (SMSF), or if an SMSF is even worth setting up in the first instance.

Negatives of Owning a Commercial Property

It is arguable as to whether the loan repayments incurred from purchasing the premises puts the business owner into a more exposed position. If interest rates were to rise, it could eat into cash flow. However, rent rises by the landlord could have the same result. Often, with a commercial property, all outgoings are paid by the tenant, so certain costs that are typically associated with owning a residential property can be lumped onto the tenant. Buying a premises does not necessarily adversely affect the business.

There are tax consequences which need to be considered, even when running a business from home. If a person claims part of their home loan as a business expense, it could undermine the capital gains tax exemption on part of the house.

It depends on a number of factors as to whether a business can, should, or must buy the premises. There is always the underlying benefit of owning an asset; this can benefit everyone, but it must not be undertaken if it could be to the detriment of the solvency and growth of the business. Whether it is a lease or purchase contract that is signed, it is always wise to seek legal advice. To determine if the property is able to be purchased and maintain a business may well require accounting advice, but bear in mind that even with the advice to buy or lease, it is the business owner that must determine if all the considerations above are congruent with the decision. These considerations can be more important than the advice.

Joint Ventures

Joint ventures are commonly used in property developments and various other commercial enterprises, including mining syndicates and research and development ventures. They are usually set up for specific purposes (rather than a long-term commercial arrangement, such as a partnership), and they can be highly profitable when you choose the right business(es) to enter into the arrangement with you. This section will not discuss partnerships, specifically, but may refer to them for comparative purposes.

There are many traps for the unwary and it is important that a joint venture is structured appropriately to achieve the desired commercial outcomes.

What is a Joint Venture?

The High Court has defined a joint venture as "an association of persons for the purposes of a particular trading, commercial, mining or other financial undertaking or endeavour with a view to mutual profit, with each participant usually (but not necessarily) contributing money, property or skill" (Source: High Court of Australia – http://www.austlii.edu.au/cgi-bin/sinodisp/au/cases/cth/HCA/1985/49.html?stem=0&synonyms=0&query=united%20dominions).

Joint ventures are often confused with partnerships, but there are some important differences, namely:

- *Joint ventures are set up for a specific purpose and generally cease to exist once that purpose is achieved, whereas partnerships are ongoing.*

- *In joint ventures, the parties maintain their status as separate entities, whereas a partnership is not a separate legal entity and every partner has unlimited liability. This is an important distinction, as in a partnership, each partner is "jointly and severally" liable for the actions of the others in all legal situations, including being criminally liable. Joint venturers are only liable to the extent stipulated in their joint venture agreement (for example, each entity is only liable for a fixed percentage of the debts of the joint venture). Getting this distinction right is also important for tax purposes.*

- *As the High Court definition implies, joint venturers can contribute "money, property or skill." In property developments, it is not uncommon for one party to provide the property or the finance, and the other to either provide the labour and skills to build the development or do the research in locating a suitable development site and undertake the feasibility as to its profitability.*

- *With joint ventures, the parties are not necessarily in a fiduciary relationship (e.g. one involving trust), whereas this is an important aspect of a partnership.*

Types of Joint Ventures

Joint ventures are generally either:

- *An 'unincorporated joint venture,' where the parties use their existing corporate structures without setting up a new business entity.*

- *An 'incorporated joint venture,' where a new entity, such as a company or a unit trust is set up to manage the joint venture. In this case, the joint venture partners are the shareholders of the new company (or unit holders of the unit trust) and the joint venturers appoint the directors of the joint venture entity. There are variations on this structure, but this is often how it works. This type of joint venture also has better asset protection for the parties, because the liabilities of the venture can be limited to the joint venture company, rather than being passed on to the joint venturers themselves.*

The type of joint venture used often depends on the scale of the operation.

Tips for the Uninitiated

In planning a joint venture, there are a number of issues which should be considered:

1. **Do proper due diligence on your proposed joint venture partner**. Have they done this before? Were they

successful? Do they have a positive existing profile in the marketplace? Are they prepared to let you speak to previous clients or joint venture partners, and if not, why not? These are just a few of the things you should consider.

2. **Get proper legal, accounting, and tax advice.** There is a lot that can go wrong if you do not structure the venture correctly.

3. **Clearly define the objectives and roles of the respective parties.** This can be done in conjunction with your professional advisors.

4. **Draw up a formal agreement.** This should cover the following issues, at least (this list is not exhaustive):

    a) the structure and objectives of the venture

    b) the management structure of the venture and their powers

    c) rights and obligations of the respective parties

    d) financial contributions, and how profits and losses will be allocated to the parties

    e) other financial issues, such as financial reporting and accountants

    f) ownership of intellectual property developed for the venture (this issue is often overlooked)

    g) marketing, and appointment of estate agents and other professionals

h) a suitable dispute resolution provision

i) exit strategies and dissolution of the venture.

5. **Maintain proper financial records**

6. **Plan regular meetings to monitor objectives and assess key performance indicators.**

Proper planning will never guarantee success, but will go a long way to mitigating the risks involved in a business venture with another party.

Commercial Leases

The law in relation to commercial and, in particular, retail leases varies from state to state. The law referred to in this section is applicable in the state of Victoria, Australia.

What are Commercial Leases?

The term 'commercial leases' is used rather loosely to refer to genuine commercial and retail leases. Retail leases are really just another type of commercial lease, which (in Victoria) relates specifically to premises used for the retailing of goods or services. Both the Law Institute of Victoria (LIV) and the Real Estate Institute of Victoria (REIV) publish commercial leases, which can be used in both retail and non-retail situations, but landlords are not required to use the standard form contracts. They may use contracts tailored to their specific needs, provided they comply with any relevant legislation.

In Victoria, general commercial leases are not governed by any specific legislation, other than the *Property Law Act 1958* (generally), while the *Retail Leases Act 2003* governs retail leases.

All states have retail tenancy legislation.

Retail Leases

Retail leasing legislation was introduced in Victoria in the mid-1980s to curb domination of the marketplace by a small group of landlords and to even the playing field for landlords and tenants alike. The current legislation relates to premises which are used "wholly or predominantly" for the retailing of goods or services, but does not include leases:

- *for less than a year*
- *where one party is a listed corporation, or subsidiary of the listed corporation*
- *where the cost of occupancy is more than $1 million a year*
- *relating to premises above the third floor of a multi-storey building, or*
- *relating to wholesaling, manufacturing, or storage businesses.*

The Retail Leases Act includes a number of important protections for tenants, including:

- *A requirement that the landlord provides a disclosure statement, outlining key provisions of the lease and the Victorian Small Business Commissioner information sheet, together with the lease agreement itself. The disclosure statement must set out the annual estimate of outgoings in relation to the lease.*

- *The tenant is entitled to a minimum five-year lease term, including renewal periods, although the tenant can waive this right.*

- *Landlords cannot recover legal expenses in relation to the costs of drafting the lease, land tax, capital costs in relation to the premises, or key money (a demand by the landlord for money to grant or transfer a lease).*

These are only some of the protections afforded by the legislation.

Not surprisingly, some landlords try and suggest that the retail tenancy legislation is not applicable to their premises, but the law is clear that if the premises are being used for retail purposes, then the relevant legislation does and will apply. This is because Australian courts and tribunals generally consider the real substance, rather than the form of a contract. The old analogy of "if it looks like a duck and quacks like a duck, then it is probably a duck" comes to mind.

Although the definition of retail premises may seem fairly clear, there can be some grey areas (for example, whether premises that are used for supplying commercial services to other businesses are covered by the legislation). The short answer (in Victoria) is that where premises are used for supplying services to other businesses, who are the "ultimate consumers" of those services, then the legislation still applies. This may come as a surprise to some landlords and tenants, who may have thought that they were parties merely to a general commercial lease. Examples of this would be the sale of shelves by a business to a retail outlet which uses them to display their goods, or the sale of ingredients to another business which makes biscuits and cakes. These would be retail sales of the shelves and ingredients, respectively.

This is just a broad overview of commercial/retail leases, as it is quite a complex area of law and is beyond the scope of this book. However, here are some guidelines for both landlords and tenants about entering into commercial leases.

Tips for Landlords:

- *Do your due diligence on any prospective tenant, including obtaining information and documentation (such as business experience and financial information in support of their application).*

- *Get personal guarantees from at least one director of tenant, if the property is being leased to a company.*

- *Make sure you comply with any applicable retail tenancy legislation.*

- *Make sure the "permitted use" of the premises is abundantly clear to the tenant and that you have appropriate planning approval for the permitted use.*

- *If necessary, get input from other parties who may be involved (for example, your lawyer, accountant, property manager, or builder).*

- *Clarify who is responsible for fit out of the premises, and who will own the fit out at the end of lease. Also, clarify that the tenant is responsible for suitable refurbishment of the premises.*

- *Obtain sufficient security by way of a security bond or bank guarantee.*

- *Ensure there is appropriate insurance for the premises,*

and that this cost can be recovered from the tenant.

- *Keep in mind that you will require the consent of a mortgagor of the property.*

Tips for Tenants:

- *Obtain appropriate legal, financial, and, if necessary, business advice. There are many traps for the unwary.*

- *Make sure the landlord has complied with any relevant retail tenancy legislation and its disclosure requirements. In particular, ensure that there has been clear disclosure of outgoings for the premises.*

- *Check whether you will need any licenses or other approvals (from the local council, for example) to run your business.*

- *Make sure the duration of the lease is adequate, including suitable options to renew for further terms. This can affect the value of your business in the event that the business is sold.*

- *Check whether there are any unusual terms in favour of the landlord in relation to demolition or renovation of the premises.*

- *Ensure that the "permitted use" adequately describes your use of the premises.*

- *Keep in mind that even if the lease is presented as "standard," you should be able to negotiate certain terms.*

Chapter 3

Conveyancing

Choosing a Conveyancer

It is imperative to engage an experienced and qualified conveyancer to peruse the Section 32 statement and advise of special conditions to best protect your interests before making an offer. This is in addition to the conveyancer's transactional role of liaising and making sure that everything happens when it needs to, from the point of signing the contract all the way through to settlement.

Most people only engage a conveyancer for that second, transactional role. However, a wise purchaser seeks advice upfront, when it can reduce their risk, save them from dealing with unnecessary concerns, and help them handle any acceptable issues. In this regard, the conveyancer's role is to help the purchaser understand that they need to undertake their own due diligence in relation to the property they are purchasing.

Talk to your potential conveyancer about the transaction, so you can make sure you are comfortable working with them. Decide whether the conveyancer is answering all of your questions satisfactorily. You should feel secure about their guidance and how they explain how, why, and when things will happen.

The real role of the conveyancer is to make things as simple and as easy as possible for the purchaser. A conveyancer that is not as experienced or qualified may cause unnecessary challenges or stress for the purchaser, especially if they are not systematic, do not follow procedures, and do not protect the best interests of their client.

The Conveyancing Process

The obligation of the conveyancer or solicitor is to ultimately ensure that they protect the interests of their client and ensure settlement takes place in accordance with the contract of sale. From that point of view, he or she becomes the liaison point linking all of the relevant parties together. Part of this role includes undertaking any necessary checks and balances to ensure that all of the purchaser's contractual obligations are complied with, including providing relevant documentation to the lender to make sure they are satisfied to move forward once they have issued mortgage documents.

It is important to work closely with your conveyancer in advance to make sure every aspect of your purchase runs smoothly.

The conveyancer also undertakes an adjustment process to ensure that the seller has paid all council and water rates, any applicable owners corporation fees, and land tax up to the day of settlement.

The process can vary considerably depending on the buyer's individual circumstances, the type of property, and the length of time to settlement. Typically, the conveyancing process starts once a contract is signed (except where a buyer has the sale documents reviewed in advance). On signing a contract, the buyer provides their representative's (conveyancer's) contact details to the sales agent, who will then forward a copy of the contract and the Section 32 vendors statement to the buyer's representative.

On receipt of the contract, the conveyancer will peruse the contract details, noting any special conditions (e.g. subject to finance) and the settlement date. The buyer would then be contacted to confirm their details and specific instructions in relation to the purchase.

The conveyancer then provides the purchaser with a number of documents to facilitate the ultimate transfer of the property.

In Victoria, these would include:

- *A cost disclosure listing all costs that may be applicable to your transaction*
- *Client authorisation, which authorises the licensed conveyancer to sign documentation on your behalf (the majority of documents are prepared and signed on the electronic conveyancing platform, PEXA/ Property Exchange Australia)*
- *State Revenue documents, which are now also online. The conveyancer will prepare the duties on the online form and email the document to you to sign.*
- *Verification of Identity instructions; all parties are required to verify their identity. This has been introduced to avoid identity theft. Australia Post is the most convenient authorised agent, however, there are also private agents who can carry out this service.*

Licensed conveyancers may also agree to process identity under certain circumstances.

Conveyancing and Property Transfers – The Basics

Conveyancing tends to be an afterthought when buying property. However, buyers can reduce the risk of their buying decision by consulting a conveyancer or solicitor before they sign a contract. A conveyancer or solicitor who takes a practical approach to the buying process can not only alert a buyer to potential traps and risks, but they can also help in the undertaking of more effective due diligence while you are searching for a property.

The approach I have taken in this chapter is to intertwine the practical reality of property transfer together with the transactional process. I hope by doing this that I can simplify and remove some of the obstacles that can arise during the buying process.

Recent History

Conveyancing is the process of transferring the legal title of property from one person or entity to another. In Australia, this process is regulated by State Government legislation. As a result, process (and practitioner qualifications), whilst delivering the same outcome, varies in each state. The commentary and tips provided in this book are predominately based on Victorian law, yet many of the concepts, fundamentals, and logic are the same in other states.

Conveyancing may be carried out by either an Australian legal practitioner or a licensed conveyancer. Deregulation of the industry in Victoria allowed independent conveyancers to begin practicing from the early 1980s. Prior to deregulation, property transfers were managed exclusively by solicitors. It is interesting to note that the Allen Report of 2005 identified the average cost of a land transfer conveyancing service in the 1970s as over $5,000. The entry of specialist conveyancers into the industry, as a result of deregulation, has resulted in a significant benefit for consumers who now enjoy conveyancing costs of around $650 to $1,600 for each transaction.

The Type of Service You Need Depends On Your Experience

As a potential buyer of property, your service requirements will vary depending on your experience, knowledge, and risk profile. Experienced buyers generally want someone to manage the process from the time of signing the contract, whilst inexperienced or first-time buyers, or those that have not bought or sold for a long time, can benefit from working with a conveyancer or solicitor before signing a contract.

Not all conveyancers and solicitors are adequately geared to provide assistance to buyers before they buy. Some will charge a fee to review a contract. I suggest engaging one that will only charge if you successfully purchase a property.

Inexperienced and experienced buyers should seriously consider getting pre-purchase advice on any purchase contract, as any contract is entered into on a buyer-beware basis. Ignorance is no defence; if you do not read or do not understand the contract, but you then sign it anyway, then it is your own fault. This is a warning that the buyer assumes the risk that he/she is buying "as is, inclusive of all defects."

Pre-purchase advice will not necessarily determine whether a property is worth buying, or whether the price is right. It is a review of the contract and vendors statement, which will assist a buyer in understanding the documents and, where relevant, give them recommendations of what further questions they might need to ask (and from whom) to reduce their risk.

Apart from any pre-purchase advice, there is also an additional approach where a conveyancer or solicitor can provide information on practical matters that are not necessarily part of the conveyancing process. This could be as simple as when to organise electricity or how to plan the collection of keys after settlement.

Buyers and sellers should also understand that an accepted offer is not binding until contracts are signed and exchanged. This is done by the agent in the state of Queensland, and in most parts of New South Wales and Victoria. Real estate agents can and will continue to market the property until there is a binding agreement. Investors should encourage their conveyancers and solicitors to ensure that exchange takes place as quickly as possible to ensure that another buyer does not swoop in and take the property, or that the buyer does not decide to buy somewhere else.

The Contract

The contract of sale is the document used to formalise the sale of real estate. It sets out the terms and conditions of the sale agreement.

Most contracts used to be standard templates, however, Consumer Affairs Victoria recently deregulated the Standard General Conditions. There is, therefore, no 'standard contract' in Victoria. A conveyancer/solicitor must check the general conditions, as they can vary. They include the set of general conditions, and also a special conditions section. The special conditions and vendors statement are tailored to each particular property and the seller's specific needs. Any special conditions are generally included for the benefit of the seller. A buyer should also insert their own special conditions into the contract to best protect their interests, if afforded the opportunity.

When a property is sold at auction, a buyer must negotiate an agreement from the seller regarding any particular conditions required *before* the auction. Due to the auction process, though, there is limited opportunity for a buyer to stipulate conditions or motivation from the seller to allow this. Any offer during auction is unconditional; there is no cooling off period.

Any property sold via a private treaty (e.g. a non-auction process) does allow the opportunity for a negotiation dialogue between the buyer, or their buyer's agent, and the seller's agent, which does provide a wider range of inclusions the buyer and seller can negotiate on. As a buyer, you can – theoretically – request the seller to provide you with a car to go with the property, but this would be unrealistic. The purpose of this example, albeit extreme, is to demonstrate that anything can be negotiated on.

Special conditions can increase obligations and costs for a buyer. They can cover a number of different things, including additional fees and costs for late settlement, and fees for contract amendments (including settlement date changes, the use of nominees for signing contracts, and limitations of vendor obligations). Special conditions also include clauses which the buyer negotiates to be inserted in the contract, such as subject to finance, subject to building and pest inspection, and gaining entry to the property prior to settlement.

If your lender does not provide with you the money to settle on the property within the agreed time of what may be 30 days, 60 days, 90 days, or 120 days (even 42 days, in New South Wales), then the vendor can charge you penalty interest.

A contract becomes unconditional once all of the buyer's obligations and conditions, such as a subject to finance clause, are met. Once a contract is unconditional, the buyer is deemed to have accepted the property in its present condition. This also includes any notices or restrictions issued over the property after the contract is signed.

Cooling Off

A buyer who signs a contract can end the contract within three clear business days from the date they sign the contract. If they have not dated the contract, it is from the date entered by the seller, which could be the same day or the next day. Not dating the contract can potentially provide the buyer with another day, depending on how quickly the seller countersigns the contract. This may also be challenged.

Whilst most buyers are aware of a cooling off period being applicable, many do not realise that a penalty applies to exercise cooling off rights. That penalty is the greater of $100 or 0.25% of the purchase price. This is why agents often collect a small holding deposit when taking an offer; as an example, this deposit could be $1000.

Cooling off does not apply to auction sales. A buyer also foregoes any right to cool off if they sign a contract either three business days before or after an advertised auction date. The right to cool off also does not apply for land used primarily for commercial or industrial purposes, for farming land larger than twenty hectares, when the parties have previously entered into a contract for the same property in similar circumstances, or where the buyer is an estate agent of a company.

It is better to be certain about the prospective property rather than rely on the ability to cool off. Some vendors will allow the agent to waive this cooling off fee at the time, but some are self-centric and will enforce this fee.

Subject to Lease or Vacant Possession

If the property is sold subject to a lease, then the current tenant is entitled to remain in the property until the expiry of the lease, provided the notice to vacate is served within the prescribed time. A buyer can only issue a notice to vacate once the contract has gone 'unconditional,' meaning that any special 'subject to' conditions included in the contract have been satisfied. This point is normally the moment when your finance is formally approved and there are no more conditions on the approval from your lender (the big condition being that valuation is satisfactory), or the point at which the agreed finance clause period has been reached. These points would typically be when the contract is subject to finance or a building inspection. If the contract is subject to vacant possession, the purchaser can negotiate to defer settlement until vacant possession is provided.

This minimum notice to vacate period can cause difficulties for a buyer, should the time for the tenant to vacate be later than the date of settlement.

Should the tenant subsequently not vacate the property until after settlement, then the buyer takes on all the responsibilities and risks of a landlord until the tenant leaves. Under these circumstances, buyers should consider landlord insurance to protect their interests.

Goods and Chattels

In the contract of sale, fittings and fixtures (items to be sold with the property) will generally be described with a general statement such as "all fixed floor coverings, window furnishings, and fixtures and fittings as inspected." If anything does not work or is damaged, it is too bad. You are buying them 'as is' (in their present state and condition, subject to fair wear and tear).

All the risk is with the purchaser in terms of the condition of the property. If you do not identify the hole in the wall hidden behind the furniture prior to sale, then you have no recourse to force the vendor to make any repairs. A special condition that could be included is that the vendor will ensure all appliances are in working order at settlement.

Buyers should add a list of items to remove any doubt on what is being sold, or not sold, with the property. The buyer should be very diligent in this regard. They should ask the selling agent for certainty in writing. If the property has a swimming pool, then the question needs to be asked if the pool cleaning equipment is included. If there is a television or speakers mounted on a wall in the entertainment area or deck, you will need to confirm if they will be removed. If items such as speakers, satellite dishes, or clotheslines are being removed, then ascertain if the wall brackets are also being taken out. If the wall brackets are being removed, confirm in writing whether the seller is going to repair and paint the walls.

A chattel is not just anything that can be picked up and removed. If the details are not included in the contract, then the buyer has no right to claim against the seller after the contract is signed. I have seen instances where dishwashers and garden sheds have been removed.

It is also well worth closely inspecting that all fixtures are in good working order (e.g. oven, stovetop, dishwasher, and heating and cooling). You might feel a little foolish checking everything, but this may well save you money in the long run. Remember that a special condition should be inserted that all fixtures are to be in working order.

Buyers should consider all of these details when considering the price they are prepared to pay for a property.

The vendor is obliged to hand over the property at settlement in the same condition as it was on the day of sale, allowing for fair wear and tear. You would also expect this to mean that the property would be clean and tidy, but in reality, some vendors do not hand over the property in an appropriate condition. This could be intentional, or it could simply be that the seller underestimated the time and effort required to move out and therefore they ran out of time.

Unfortunately, purchasers do not have a great deal of leverage to delay settlement should the property not be in the expected condition and there is no obligation for the vendor to provide the property in a clean and tidy state. The purchaser cannot delay settlement or withhold monies at settlement. The purchaser's only right is to "settle reserving their rights." What this means is, after settlement, perhaps the buyer can attempt to make a claim against the vendor. However, issuing proceedings against the vendor is expensive and time-consuming with no guarantee of a positive outcome.

What is 'fair wear and tear?' This refers to any deterioration that is part of the normal pattern of property ownership. A purchaser has to accept the property in the deteriorated condition. An example of this principle is a hot water service that breaks down during the contract period (the period between signing the contract and settlement). The purchaser might argue that the vendor should replace the hot water service to return the property to the condition in which it was sold. However, to do so would, in fact, place the property in a better condition than when it was sold. Such an event is part of the normal pattern of home ownership and therefore lies within the determination of fair wear and tear. The seller cannot be forced to replace the hot water service.

Buying at Auction

If you are purchasing a property at an auction, or making an offer either three business days before or after the advertised auction date, the primary consideration is that you have no cooling off rights. If you win the auction, you are locked into the contract and have no option to exit. If, for any reason, you cannot eventually complete the contract, then you would lose the deposit and potentially be sued for other costs and any shortfall in price from a subsequent sale. Buyers need to have done their due diligence before the day of the auction.

Due diligence includes any matter to do with the property; any building inspections, price research, and borrowing capacity. Buyers should discuss with their lender the difference between pre-approval and full approval before committing themselves to an auction. Any special consideration required needs to be agreed upon with the selling agent before the auction. That might include a variation in the amount of the deposit to be paid, or the timing of settlement, whether that be 30 days, 60 days, 90 days, or any other period.

If you are considering having a building or a pest inspection done, you need to do that before the auction. This gives the relevant parties enough time to provide feedback and determine some common ground.

Negotiating a Contract

Sale by negotiation provides a buyer greater flexibility in negotiating conditions to suit their particular needs and circumstances. This can reduce a buyer's risk should they eventually be successful in securing the property. However, where at an auction a buyer can see their competition, a buyer has no visibility of competing offers that might also be under negotiation.

Negotiating a contract can allow a buyer to propose their own terms and conditions for the seller's consideration. Apart from the price, this can also include the amount of deposit, inclusion of finance and inspection clauses, the settlement date, and any other factors relevant for the buyer.

Buying Off-the-Plan Property

Buying off-the-plan property has additional risks, however these risks can be largely eliminated by engaging a specialist buyer advocate. Off-the-plan means that you are buying a property that does not exist at the time of signing the contract. This could be anything from a block of vacant land to an apartment in a 500-unit building.

The risks of buying off-the-plan are numerous; most importantly, the value of the property may change from the time the contract is signed to the time of settlement. This presents considerable risk for a buyer if market values decline over time, which they often do for high rise apartments, in particular, irrespective of the growth in the suburb.

The difficulty here is that a lender cannot value the property until it has been completed. When it is land being sold, completion is when all infrastructure has been built and the subdivision is submitted for registration. In the instance of a building, the lender will not value the property until construction is complete and a Certificate of Occupancy has been issued.

Sometimes, depending on market conditions, the lender's valuation can be substantially less than the contract price. When this happens, the buyer must either walk away from the contract, losing their deposit, or find the additional money from another source.

Only conditional finance approval can be available at the time of signing an off-the-plan contract, and this cannot be relied upon. You may become injured and unable to work; therefore you are unable to service the loan repayments on the proposed loan, and thus you are not offered finance when you require it. You may be terminated from your job, and have no employment when you need finance. Your current relationship, and lending capacity, may no longer exist when settlement finally arrives. Once again, if the buyer cannot provide sufficient funds to complete the purchase, they are likely to lose their deposit.

The additional difficulty here is that, for off-the-plan properties, settlement date generally falls due two weeks after the property has been registered (given its own title). If there is a shortfall of funds, based on the valuation, then there is less than a two-week window for the buyer to find the additional money.

Off-the-plan contracts also include a 'sunset clause' or a 'registration period.' These clauses provide a timeline for completion of the development; however, this timeframe is often quite extensive (the timeframe can be up to sixty months). Effectively, this means that, irrespective of the expected date of completion (registration) indicated by the selling agent, completion may be as far away as the time noted in the sunset clause (registration period). We have witnessed delays of land registration by as much as fifteen months from the date originally indicated in the contract.

Where delays occur, the buyer needs to review their living arrangements if they plan to move in immediately, and this can be difficult in terms of re-negotiating rental agreements. If the end of the registration period is reached, then either the seller or the buyer can cancel the contract.

I have seen contracts cancelled by the developer, intentionally, because the area has increased in value dramatically. The developer has exercised the sunset clause, cancelled the contract, and then put all the apartments back on the market the next day at a much higher price. Think about all the interest the buyer would have paid on their deposit of 10%, paid four years earlier.

If an off-the-plan purchase includes construction, buyers need to be aware that they are putting their complete trust in the nominated builder for the quality of works. It is wise to diligently check the builder's credentials by inspecting any work they have previously completed. You would like to think that the builder or developer would pay attention to defects quite promptly and efficiently, but this is not always the case.

With off-the-plan, the developer generally has what is called a 'variation limit,' which means that they can vary the plans by up to 5%, based on council instructions. There may also be a clause that allows the developer to substitute goods and fittings with something of the same quality if the specified ones are not available at the time. This essentially means you might not get exactly what you thought you were.

There is a proposal before parliament, at the time of writing this book, to change the sunset legislation. As it is now, the vendor can cancel the contract at the end of the registration period (up to as many as sixty months), return the deposit, and sell the property for much more. The new proposal would allow vendors to terminate contracts, but they must provide warning of intent and proper cause to terminate. They cannot just stall. The purchaser may have the right to reject the termination, unless no building has commenced.

Signing the Contract

When signing a contract, you should always print your full name so that it is consistent with the name noted on your primary identification documents. Your name should be the same on the contract, the mortgage documents, and any other documents associated with your property purchase. Middle names that do not match, or only printing an initial of a middle name, must be supported with sufficient ID for many lenders.

Any mortgage documents issued with incorrect or incomplete names cannot be amended. Lenders will cancel the mortgage documents and reissue them with the correct names. The reissue of mortgage documents can cause delays in settlement, and under this circumstance, the purchaser could suffer financial penalties imposed by the seller under the terms of the contract.

It is important to always use your full legal name, as per your birth certificate, passport, and driver's license. Many people have nicknames, or names that they go by, but to become a legal owner you must use your full, legal name.

You should also take care to use your normal signature, as signatures are cross checked on all documents at various stages throughout the process. If signatures do not match, settlement can be delayed.

Deposit Money

Deposit money is paid into the selling agent's trust account, and is held in this account until settlement has taken place or it is released to the vendor under Section 27 of the state legislation act (in Victoria).

The deposit money can be released from the trust account to the seller before settlement, with the buyer's consent, by filling out the relevant form. This form is often presented to a buyer at the time of signing the contract. Buyers should not sign the release of the deposit at this stage, and the form should simply be passed on to their conveyancer or solicitor. In order to release the deposit with a degree of safety, the seller must demonstrate, through the provision of a letter of evidence from their lender, that the amount required to discharge the mortgage is not more than 80% of the sale price, that there is no facility to redraw on the loan to an amount in excess of 80% of the sale price, and that they are not in default under the terms of the loan.

Nominations

If the intended owner, or owners, of a property is not present to sign the contract, then the party signing the contract should sign using their own name and add the term "and/or nominee."

That means that while party A may sign the contract, the actual ownership will eventually go to party A and party B. Or party A signs it, and ownership goes to two completely different parties, B and C. These are called nominations, where the people signing the contract declare that when the transfer goes through, the property will belong to someone who was not a signatory to the contract. A buyer's agent may do this, if attending an auction on the buyer's behalf (if the buyer cannot be present). It is best to inform the selling agent and obtain their consent for you to do this. There must be a relationship to nominate to avoid stamp duty implications. The purchase contract could be signed initially in one entity name (e.g. a trust or self-managed super fund, or a sibling, husband, or wife). In these cases, a relationship has more chance of being demonstrated.

Where possible, it is preferred that the intended owners sign the contract. Some contracts contain a special condition allowing the vendor's representative to charge the buyer an additional fee for using a nomination. This is not a set fee, however, I have seen instances where the fee is as high as $500. A buyer's conveyancer or solicitor may also charge a fee for preparation and lodgement of nomination documents.

Buyers should be aware that a nomination, such as these examples described above, is deemed to be a transfer in the state of Queensland. As such, both the party named on the contract and the nominated final owner will pay stamp duty (i.e. there will be two lots of stamp duty paid). This can also be the case in New South Wales.

Negotiating an Offer

Buyers can negotiate a purchase if the property is not being sold at auction. The following details should be considered for inclusion in any offer, however, it should be noted that the negotiation process can still be competitive and offers with numerous conditions could put you at a disadvantage in comparison to less restrictive offers.

Time Limit

Put a time limit on the offer, so that the selling agent has a firm timeline in which to consult the vendor and respond to the offer.

Price and Deposit

Know the price you are prepared to pay, including the amount of deposit. Deposits are normally 5–10%. More often, the common figure is becoming 5%, with the exception of off-the-plan properties, for which deposits are always 10%. On occasion, a vendor may also accept a 'deposit guarantee' from a bank, rather than an actual deposit payment.

Settlement Day

Specify a particular day for settlement, rather than noting the number of days to settlement (typically 30 days, 60 days, or 90 days). It is prudent to plan settlement on any business day except for a Friday. Where possible, a buyer should plan not to move into the property on the day of settlement. Most settlements occur in the afternoon, therefore keys are not normally available until mid to late afternoon.

Despite all efforts, settlements can sometimes be delayed, and whilst a delay may only be a matter of thirty minutes, some settlements cannot be completed on the same day if there is a more serious reason for a delay. Considerable delays can now be experienced due to PEXA. If your settlement is postponed to another day, then it generally moves to the next business day. If your settlement date is a Friday, this could be moved to Monday and you lose the weekend.

One example I can give you is a Friday settlement which was scheduled for 4:00pm, but the buyer's bank did not allocate funds by the prescribed settlement time. In this instance, the vendor agreed to still allow the buyer to access the property under a license agreement on the Saturday. However a seller is not obliged to agree to allowing access, irrespective of the circumstances. If this settlement had been arranged for the Thursday, it would have mitigated the risk attached to the delay.

Finance Clause

Finance approval is dependent on the lender valuing the property and, therefore, a buyer's individual circumstances may require any offer to be made subject to finance approval. When making an offer subject to finance, it is prudent to nominate a lender by name (e.g. ANZ, CBA, NAB, Westpac) or alternately use the term "an authorised deposit-taking institution" (ADI). ADIs include banks, building societies, and credit unions.

A finance clause also provides for the nomination of a minimum amount required in order to be able to complete the contract. Nominating a minimum amount provides a safety valve for the buyer in the event that the lender's valuation is low. Where a low valuation applies, the lender may not provide funding to the minimum amount noted in the contract.

A date by which the finance approval is to be obtained also needs to be specified. Typically, a selling agent (remembering they only serve the seller, not the buyer) will attempt to recommend that the finance clause is subject to approval within seven days of the buyer signing the contract. In order to provide finance approval, a lender will value the property. The process of assessing a loan application, ordering a valuation, and then a review of the valuation and final assessment can often take more than seven days. A 14- or 21-day timeframe is a more suitable option for the purpose of receiving finance approval.

Should finance approval not be received by the due date, it is possible to seek an extension to the approval date. In the majority of cases, a vendor will accept a request for extension to the finance approval date to avoid the contract coming to an end.

When signing a contract subject to finance, the buyer must do everything possible to obtain finance. A letter of decline from a lender must be provided in order to exit a contract under this clause. Buyers should have consulted with their mortgage broker in advance of signing a contract in order to have the finance approval provided in a timely fashion.

Building Inspections

Would you buy a car without at least starting the engine, or would you invest in a racehorse without a veterinary check? The same principles apply when buying any property with a building or dwelling. The building may seem structurally sound, however, it is difficult to determine the real integrity of a building without having a property inspection.

The purpose of undertaking a building inspection is to check the structural integrity of the building, and to reduce the risk associated with the purchase.

Inspections can often reveal issues with a building that are not easily identifiable to an untrained eye. I knew a buyer who considered bidding at an auction for a property quoted in a range above $1 million. The buyer decided at the last minute to engage a building inspector to check the property. The inspection was conducted the day before the auction, and revealed that the building needed underpinning with a potential cost of $200,000. This additional potential cost would have pushed the total expense over the buyer's limit. Therefore, he decided to leave this property and continue his search for alternatives.

The standard inspection clause included in a contract provides an opportunity for a buyer to end the contract should the inspection reveal a major structural defect, or major pest infestation in the case of pest inspections. Buyers can gain additional protection by removing the reliance on the wording of major structural defects or major pest infestations, making the contract "subject to major defects" or, even better, "subject to the purchaser's satisfaction." A buyer's solicitor or conveyancer can provide more specific advice in relation to a satisfactory clause for each individual circumstance.

Any offer including a subject to inspection clause should also note a timeframe for completion of the inspection. This is typically seven days after signing a contract, although this does not apply when a contract is signed at an auction. When properties are sold at auction, the buyer must have the inspection completed before the auction if they are going to get one done, as it is not possible to make an auction contract subject to an inspection.

It is also worth noting that building inspectors are generally not qualified to conduct pest inspections and, likewise, pest inspectors are usually not able to conduct building inspections.

Building inspections do not generally cover in-depth inspections of electrical works or plumbing; specialists in these fields would need to be engaged accordingly. This is advisable, especially on an older property. However, defects associated with these areas are not considered structural defects.

The Section 32 (Victoria) – Vendors Statement

This document is provided by the seller to all potential buyers. The statement requires the seller to provide information to a purchaser before the contract is signed. It is a disclosure statement. The vendor is only required to disclose certain aspects regarding the property.

The principle of 'buyer beware' applies, even with the provision of this document, as it is a statement of fact and not necessarily a statement of compliance. The content of a Section 32 is also limited in scope and does not cover all elements in respect to the property. It certainly does not provide an indication of price. Even with the Section 32, buyers should take the time to understand the content and conduct further inquiries should the information not be to their satisfaction.

What is in the Section 32?

The Section 32 will consist of a summary of the relevant information in the first few pages, followed by a number of supporting documents used to substantiate the summary.

The information provided consists of the following details.

Statutory Warnings to the Buyer

Any warnings or notices issued to the current owners should be declared in the Section 32. This would include any advertised planning applications for neighbouring properties or notices in relation to illegal building works, but only if an order has been issued.

The Seller's Details

The seller would normally be the owner of the property, although under certain circumstances the seller can be another authorised individual or entity. The details of the seller's right to sell must be included in the Section 32.

The owner is identified in the 'Register Search Statement,' or evidence is provided as to their right to sell. The Register Search Statement is a copy of the property record provided by the Land Titles office. The statement includes the identity of the property, the owner, and any encumbrances, covenants, and caveats affecting the property.

The identity of the property is described by a Volume number and an associated Folio number. The property is shown on a corresponding diagram of the plan of subdivision by a Lot number.

Where a car park has a separate title, it will have independent and unique Volume and Folio numbers. If this applies, both the Volume and Folio numbers of the primary property and the car park must be noted in the contract.

Financial Details

The financial details aggregate the normal annual cost of rates or fees attached to the property, plus any potential land tax obligation where the property is not the seller's principal place of residence.

The financials include council and water rates (not including water and sewerage usage costs), and any owners corporation fees.

Insurance

Whilst the vendor is legally obligated to maintain insurance over the property to the day of settlement, there is no way of ensuring that this is the case. If the property is not insured or inadequately insured, and a major event such as a fire occurs, the purchaser can sue the vendor accordingly. If the vendor does not have insurance, this would result in the purchaser appointing a solicitor to initiate litigation, and they would have to wait for the court's verdict to recover costs. If insurance is in place, then immediately initiated repairs could occur and the insurer could recover costs either directly from the vendor or from the vendor's insurance.

Where a property is not insured by an owners corporation, a buyer should consider insuring the building as soon as possible.

Land Use – Restrictions

'Encumbrance' is the term used to describe a claim that one person or entity has against another person's land. An encumbrance is a claim against the land and not a claim on the owner. Therefore, if the land changes ownership, the new owner takes both the land and any encumbrance attached to the land. A Section 173 agreement (an agreement with an owner of land to set out conditions or restrictions on the use or development of the land, or to achieve planning objectives on the land established by a council) is also an encumbrance.

Covenants are restrictions recorded against the property. Covenant restrictions can include limitations on the number of dwellings permitted or even the type of building materials that are permitted on the land. These restrictions are independent of and additional to planning restrictions noted in council zoning regulations.

Details of any encumbrances and covenants are normally noted on, and attached with, the Register Search Statement.

Bushfire

A declaration is made on whether the land is in, or not in, a designated bushfire-prone area. When a property is in a designated bushfire-prone area, a buyer could determine the significance of this by contacting the council. On occasions where a property is in a designated bushfire-prone area, special building provisions may apply for any development on the land. Special building provisions may be minimal, but they can also be quite extensive and onerous on a buyer. Some rural properties, for instance, may have a requirement for a 15,000 litre underground water tank for firefighting purposes.

Road Access

This is a declaration that the property is accessible by road.

As a separate declaration, a vendors statement could include a statement to confirm whether there are any road proposals requiring any part of the property.

Planning and Zoning

There are numerous planning zones determined by councils, and whilst the zoning is stipulated, it is up to the buyer to check any limitations created by the listed zone. Council Planning and Building departments can provide more specific information, particularly where a buyer might be considering extending or replacing the current building.

Planning information also includes details of any overlays affecting the property. Whilst most overlays do not have a significant impact, a buyer would benefit from consulting with council about the relevant details. Historical significance overlays, in particular, can place onerous restrictions on a property. A purchaser should make enquiries as to the planning and overlays to ensure the intended use and enjoyment of the property will be permitted.

Notices

Any notices previously issued to the vendor should be included. This could include property management plans, reports, or orders in respect to the land. It should also include any details issued by council in relation to planning permit applications for adjoining properties.

Building Permits Issued in the Last Seven Years

A seller is required to provide the details of any building permits issued for the property in the last seven years, where a permit has been issued, and – depending on the extent of the works – the vendors statement could also be required to include a Certificate of Final Inspection or Occupancy and a copy of any Builders Warranty insurance applicable to the work undertaken.

If any extensions have been added, but they are not stated, they would be over seven years old, and it is best to seek confirmation from council that they are legal additions. A vendor is not required to disclose works that have not been permitted. The purchaser may make enquiries with the building department of the relevant council if they are concerned that works may have been carried out without a council permit. These enquiries may initiate an inspection by council and a subsequent order or notice issued. Any order or notice issued after the date of the contract becomes the responsibility of the purchaser.

Particulars of Any Owner-Builder Works

If building works of more than $16,000 have been undertaken in the last seven years by an Owner-Builder, rather than a registered builder, then the Owner-Builder must provide, in addition to the Building Permit, a copy of current Owner-Builder insurance and an Owner-Builder Report not more than three months old. A building permit may not exist, and the vendor is not required to obtain or provide it.

The Owner-Builder Report is a report undertaken by an authorised building inspector to confirm the quality and compliance of the works.

Notices or Orders Issued by Authorities

Disclosure of any notices or orders issued including fencing, road widening, sewerage, or planning applications for adjoining properties.

Owners Corporation Details

A property is automatically subject to an owners corporation if the plan of subdivision includes any common property. An owners corporation (formerly Body Corporate) is defined by Consumer Affairs Victoria as the "manager of common property." The owners corporation must manage, administer, repair, and maintain the common property for the benefit and enjoyment of the owners.

The administration function includes building insurance (owners may elect to take out their own building insurance) and a public liability insurance over the common property.

In most instances, professional management companies are appointed for this purpose. However, on occasion, for smaller developments of four or less properties, the owners operate the owners corporation on their own behalf. Two-lot sites may be exempt from insurance obligations; owners must insure common property with their building insurance.

Where owners corporations are self-managed, buyers should ensure insurance is in place on both the building and the common property. If insurance is not in place, it is then the responsibility of the purchaser to arrange their own insurance.

The cost and benefit of any public liability insurance, theoretically, can be shared by all owners. However, where there is no appointed manager, any new buyer would need to negotiate with the other owners in order to have them contribute to the public liability insurance.

Public liability insurance provides protection in the event that a person suffers an injury whilst on the common property. Where no insurance is in place, the individual lot owners could be sued for damages if an injury occurs.

Service Connections

Any services of electricity, gas, water, sewerage, or telephone which are *not connected* are listed. Where services are not connected, any connection costs would be the responsibility of the buyer. Not all services are necessarily available for connection on all properties. Some lenders will not lend on a property if services are not connected, or cannot be connected.

Supporting Documents

Supporting documents are included as attachments to the

Section 32 vendors statement to validate the information.

Register Search Statement

The Register Search Statement reflects the record of the property held by Land Victoria (for Victorian properties). It details the land description, including the Volume and Folio numbers, and the lot and plan of subdivision details.

Also listed is the name(s) of the owner(s) of the property, the name of any mortgagee that holds an interest over the property, if there are covenants or a caveat registered on the property, and if the property is subject to an owners corporation.

Caveats

A caveat is a document that any person with a legal interest in a property can lodge at Land Victoria (for Victorian properties). After recording, a caveat note appears on the title giving anyone with interest notice that a third party claims rights over the property (Source: Department of Environment, Land, Water and Planning – http://www.dtpli.vic.gov.au/property-and-land-titles/land-titles/dealing-with-titles/caveats-covenants-and-easements).

A caveat prevents the registration of a further dealing with the land that affects the person who has lodged the caveat, unless that person has consented to the dealing or if the caveat has lapsed, is cancelled, is removed, or is withdrawn by the caveator.

The most common circumstance for lodging a caveat on a property is where a couple is married or are in a de facto relationship where the property is registered in only one name, and the other partner lodges a caveat to prevent the registered owner selling the property without their knowledge and subsequent approval.

Caveats must be withdrawn either before or at the time of settlement.

Plan of Subdivision

The plan of subdivision is a diagrammatic representation of the land including dimensions, any easements over the land, and the common property (where common property exists). Where the property is an apartment or unit in a large complex, the plan of subdivision would identify all parts of the property (such as car parks or storage spaces). These can be identified as part of the primary property, or they can have their own unique Volume and Folio identifiers.

Easements

An easement is a non-possessory right of use and right of entry onto land owned by another person. An easement could exist on a property where the Water Authority has reserved a portion of the land for water and sewer infrastructure. An easement of this nature can place limitations on future building plans, as permission would be required from the relevant authority to build over the easement.

Owners Corporation Search Report

This report shows the total number of lots subject to an owners corporation, and the liability share of each lot for fees and costs belonging to the owners corporation.

Planning Certificate or Planning Report

The planning certificate lists the zoning of the property and any overlays as determined by council. Your council's building and planning department, or a town planner, can offer further relevant information specific to the property on any zoning or overlay details.

Zoning and overlays are particularly important should a buyer be considering any form of development or subdivision of the land.

Council Land Information Certificate

The content of a council Land Information Certificate varies between councils. Primarily, the certificate confirms the annual rates applicable to the property, any information as applicable on parking permits, flood levels, and termite infestation, and any outstanding notices on the property.

This certificate does not provide planning or building information.

On occasion, this certificate is replaced by a copy of a current rates notice. Whilst the rates notice confirms the annual rates applicable, it does not provide any other information that is normally included in the Land Information Certificate.

Council Building Certificate

This certificate provides information on any planning or building permits issued in the last seven years. Where applicable, the certificate will also include information where a Certificate of Final Inspection or Certificate of Occupancy has been required, and subsequently whether all certificates have been issued in accordance with the permits.

This certificate is a statement of fact, and not necessarily one of compliance. Therefore, buyers should be wary if an inspection of the property indicates that works not noted in the Building Certificate are evident.

The purchaser assumes any future liability for any illegal

building works and, therefore, where there is any possibility of illegal building works, the buyer should consider title insurance as added protection. It is estimated that as many as 30% of freestanding dwellings in Victoria have some form of illegal building works. If there is any doubt, title insurance can provide some protection against any future costs resulting from illegal building works.

Owner Corporation Certificate

This certificate provides a range of relevant information in relation to the owners corporation, including the annual fees and any additional levies that have been struck (invoiced) for maintenance or repair works. Levies can be struck to cover the cost of any significant works not covered in the normal annual budget. Any levies struck after the signing of a contract become the responsibility of the purchaser, as the money raised by the levy will contribute to works which the buyer will benefit from in the future.

This certificate can also provide information on future repair works which will impact the buyer. For example, imagine the owners corporation certificate includes details about future repair works over the next three to five years. However, potential buyers who are not familiar with the documentation in the vendors statement may miss this detail. In this instance, the repairs may result in an additional levy of $4,000 per year for the next four years. That would mean an additional cost of $16,000 to the purchaser. That is not to say that the property is not a good property to buy. It may well be, but the buyer would need to take these future costs into consideration when calculating the price they are prepared to pay.

Transfer of Land

This document is used by the Land Registrar to record the details of any change in ownership. The document lists the seller and buyer's names, the reason for the transfer, and any financial consideration paid. It also records the 'manner of holding' for the buyers. This document is now prepared electronically.

Manner of Holding

This describes the type of ownership of a property where there is more than one owner to be listed on the title.

Joint Proprietors

The general type of ownership is joint proprietors, meaning an equal ownership share. Under joint proprietorship, when one of the owners dies, their share of the property automatically passes on to the surviving owner. This is the most common type of ownership for married partners or de facto relationships.

Tenants in Common

If two people are buying a property, it is important to be clear about whether they are buying it as "joint proprietors" or "tenants in common." Joint proprietors automatically own equal shares. Tenants in common is generally used when a property is not going to be the principal place of residence for either party. It may be an investment property and, for tax purposes, it may be beneficial to have the majority of the property owned in one party's name. Seek advice on this, as you would with anything else in this book. Tenants in common properties could be 90% owned by person A and 10% owned by person B, or each party could own a 50% share each.

Under ownership as tenants in common, if one of the owners dies, their share of the property does not automatically pass to the other owner. Rather, it passes in accordance with their will. They could leave their share of the property to a charity (the RSPCA, as an example), to a family member, or even to their dog or cat.

If people purchase using tenants in common ownership, they need to have their will up to date.

Verification of Identity

The Victorian State Government has legislated that all participants (buyers and sellers) in property settlements are legally required to be identified. Your conveyancer has the responsibility to ensure you complete the required VOI (Verification of Identity). This legislation has been introduced to limit title fraud. This identification process is different to that required by lenders; the identification documents are also not necessarily the same as those required to obtain the 100 points of identification used for other purposes.

Stamp Duties

The Duties Online form incorporates all previous SRO (State Revenue Office) forms, and also enables the SRO to identify when the buyer is a foreign purchaser (an additional duty of 3% then applies).

Stamp Duty Concessions

Buyers, if so entitled, generally receive the benefit of stamp duty concessions at the time of settlement. However, buyers should budget to provide full stamp duty at settlement, as some lenders rebate the duty after settlement. Rebates have been reduced.

When a buyer is building a new property, in certain circumstances, the full stamp duty saving is received after construction is complete. This option is not available to everyone.

Lenders will generally quote full stamp duty rates up to the day before settlement. Part of the conveyancer's role is to ensure that the lender updates the stamp duty payable inclusive of the concession rate at the time of settlement.

For 'Love and Affection' transfers, stamp duty was previously not applicable to investment or commercial property, but stamp duty is now payable (in Victoria). Love and Affection transfers can still apply to the principal place of residence, where no stamp duty is applicable. It is best you obtain advice as to who falls under love and affection; commonly, it is the de facto or married partner of the person.

First-Home Buyers

If you are a first-home buyer and the property is going to be your principal place of residence, you may qualify for a reduction or elimination of stamp duty, depending on when you purchase it, where the property is located, and the price.

Principal Place of Residence Stamp Duty Concession

Any buyer that is buying a property as their principal place of residence, depending on location and price, may be entitled to a stamp duty concession.

Financial Statement

The pre-settlement financial statement includes a summary of the amount outstanding after adjustments, funds being provided by the lender (where there is a lender), and any additional funding requirements.

Where a buyer is contributing additional funds for final settlement, it is best practice to have the lender draw these funds from a nominated account held with that lender. If this arrangement is not in place, the buyer is required to provide the balance at settlement to a conveyancer/solicitor's trust account or PEXA suspense account.

Adjustments

The statement of adjustments is prepared so that neither the buyer nor the seller bears the expense, or gains the benefit, of the income for a period when they were not the owner.

Items adjusted are expenses or income of a recurring nature, which typically include expenses such as council rates, water rates, owners corporation fees, land tax (in certain instances), and rental income. The method of adjustment provides that the vendor shall pay the rates until settlement, and the purchaser shall bear the rates from the day of settlement.

As an example, assume that council rates (charged annually on a financial year basis, from July 1st to June 30th the following year) are $4,000, and settlement falls on the 31st of December:

a) the vendor should pay the full amount of $4,000 in advance of settlement.

b) the purchaser pays to the vendor at settlement for the period from January 1st to June 30th (one half on the billing period). The purchaser therefore pays $2,000 to the vendor. This amount is additional to the balance of the purchase price owing.

If the seller has not paid the $4,000 in advance of settlement, the full amount not paid is deducted from the selling amount owed to the vendor, and a cheque is then forwarded to the relevant authority (in this example, the cheque would be paid to the council).

The overall impact is illustrated as follows:

Purchase price
$550,000

Deposit paid
$50,000

Balance due
$500,000

Adjusted Council rates (to be paid by purchaser)
$2,000

Balance to be paid at settlement
$502,000

If Council rates ($4,000) have not been paid, cheques drawn at settlement will be:

To the seller
$498,000

To the council
$4,000

Total
$502,000

Note: owners corporation levies, which are non-recurring, are not adjustable. However, the obligation to pay any levy is based on the date of the contract of sale, such that any levy struck before the contract date is the responsibility of the seller and for any levy struck after the day of sale, the responsibility lies with the purchaser.

Settlement

Leading up to settlement, the purchaser must contact their preferred electricity and gas supplier to organise those services to be connected to their name. The conveyancer does the same for council, the water authority, and, where applicable, any owners corporation.

Up to seven days before settlement, the purchaser is entitled to undertake a pre-settlement inspection of the property. The purpose of this inspection is to ensure that the property is largely in the same condition as it was on the day they signed the contract. If the buyer locates damage, they can report this to their conveyancer. The inspection is not a time to find faults or defects that were not checked prior to signing the contract. As an example, if there was a hole in a wall that was hidden by some furniture or a wall mounted television at the time of signing the contract, the buyer has no right to have the wall repaired at the seller's cost if the hole is evident during the pre-settlement inspection.

The purchaser is also, to a large degree, at the mercy of the goodwill of the vendor in terms of the cleanliness of the property at the time of settlement.

There is always the opportunity to have significant issues addressed and corrected before settlement. Your conveyancer will provide specific advice depending on the issue and circumstances.

Buyers and sellers are not required to attend settlement. Settlements are managed by the conveyancers and solicitors on behalf of their clients. The conveyancer is the gatekeeper, conducting the exchange of the funds and documents with the banks.

On settlement day, a buyer (or their rental manager, if purchasing an investment property) can collect keys from the selling agent's office once settlement is confirmed. Settlements generally occur in the afternoon; therefore, buyers should plan to collect keys during the mid to late afternoon of the day of settlement.

Once settlement is agreed and confirmed, the vendor's conveyancer will contact the selling agent to confirm settlement and authorise the handover of keys. The buyer can collect the keys to their new property once this has been done.

After settlement, the buyer's conveyancer notifies the council, the owners corporation (where applicable), the State Revenue Office, and the water authority of the change in ownership.

A New Consideration – Title Insurance

Title insurance can be used as a risk management tool in the conveyancing transaction.

The title insurer assists in resolving issues, and providing compensation, in cases of boundary misalignment (incorrect fence positioning), unsatisfied conditions of planning permits, and illegal building works.

As I previously mentioned, it has been reported that as many as 30% of pre-existing, freestanding properties in Victoria have illegal building works on them, which could be as small as a deck or as large as a full extension on the property. Any issues that arise from illegal building works are the responsibility of the current owner and there is no ability to pursue a previous owner for compensation. Title insurance provides peace of mind where any potentially illegal building works exist on a property.

Title insurance is a one-off expense for the life of ownership of the property. Generally, for a property of up to $500,000 in value, it only costs approximately $400, which makes it very economical.

In Summary

Using a conveyancer is important and almost always necessary for a purchase, as discussed. Here is a summary of reasons why:

- *Timely settlement to avoid penalties charged by the vendor*

- *Any problems with paperwork, title, contract, and documents are addressed appropriately and in a timely fashion.*

- *Drafting of special conditions to protect the interests of the buyer, such as subject to finance, property inspection and pest inspection, and even subject to due diligence to the buyer's satisfaction (although the latter could be construed as too vague for the vendor)*

- *Determination of entitlements and any adjustments for costs such as rates, so no liability travels with the property*

- *Assistance with the completion of forms*
- *Ensures all costs and disbursements are accurately accounted for*
- *Ensures that titles are registered correctly, in the correct ownership structure and percentages*
- *Determination and advice on any negative or limiting factors, or factors the buyer should be aware of such as:*
    - Environmental limitations or overlays
    - Covenants
    - Easements
    - Boundaries
    - Caveats.

Buying Interstate? The Information You Need to Know

As many property investors know, the city you currently call home is not always the best place to invest in.

You have done your research; picked out the potential growth areas, drawn up your budget and growth expectations, and are now preparing to invest interstate. But there are many steps to the buying process, and they can differ from state to state. Here are some key differences in purchasing properties interstate.

Inspecting A Property

Assuming that you have picked out the area and property type you want to purchase, the next step is inspecting potential properties. **Victorian** investors will be aware of Section 32, a mandatory vendors statement, which provides buyers with a range of information about the property before the sale. The Section 32 document is prepared by a lawyer, conveyancer, or by the vendor under legal instruction. If the vendor knowingly provides any false information, they have committed a criminal offence and will face fines. The document will include any mortgages or debts charged against the land, planning information, disclosure of services connected to the property, and any permitted building work that has been carried out in the last seven years. Registered building works may be covered under warranty for six years, even if the property has changed hands multiple times. Section 32 is generally considered the most comprehensive vendor disclosure statement in the country, and must be provided before the auction or before a contract is signed in a private sale.

In **New South Wales**, sellers are required to provide Schedule 1 Prescribed Documents, but these generally only include mortgages on the property, deeds and restrictions on the use of land, and a Section 149 (2) planning certificate from the local council. Fair Trading NSW recommend that buyers carry out an independent pre-purchase inspection report. A prudent conveyancer should inspect the local council files to ensure that all structures on the property are compliant. The local council will issue a Building Certificate, which will allow a seven-year exemption from action by the council on all structures currently standing on the property. The cost of a Building Certificate, including a council inspection of the property, will have a cost in the vicinity of $250. It is also prudent to ensure that any pool is fully compliant with the local laws.

Your inspection report should be carried out by a licensed builder, surveyor, or architect. Make sure they have professional indemnity cover, in case you want to seek compensation for any errors they make. You will have to weather the cost of the report yourself, which will vary depending on the consultant and the size, age, and condition of the property. The report will not cover information on any hidden or structural problems with the property, as it is generally just a visual assessment. It also will not cover electrical wiring, plumbing or gasfitting, or fireplaces and chimneys. If you are concerned about any aspect of the property in particular, you should engage a specialised inspector before purchasing.

Sellers in **South Australia** are required to provide a Form 1 disclosure statement to the purchaser through the seller's real estate agent. The Form 1 must be available to buyers before the auction date. If a property is being sold through a private sale, the Form 1 must be provided at least ten days prior to the settlement date. The provision of the Form 1 also affects a buyer's cooling off period. A Form 1 generally covers similar information to New South Wales' Schedule 1 Prescribed Documents, so an independent inspection report is recommended.

Queensland currently does not have a compulsory disclosure statement for all residential properties. Body corporates should provide information for townhouses, apartments, and units. The Queensland Office of Fair Trading advises buyers to carry out independent inspections. The same goes for buyers looking to invest in **Tasmania** or in the **Northern Territory**, after vendor disclosure legislation was dumped in 2012. Sellers in **Western**

Australia are not required to provide a disclosure statement to any prospective buyers, but should prepare a Seller's Disclosure Statement for their agent.

It is important to note that in standard form **Queensland** contracts, time is of the essence. This means that if you cannot settle on settlement day, you are at risk of losing your deposit and being sued for damages. There is no leeway, so if you are signing a contract, make sure the dates for finance, settlement, and other important issues are well within your time budgets.

When selling property in the **Australian Capital Territory**, vendors are required to provide documents prior to sale including an assessment of the physical condition of the property, an asbestos assessment report, and any restrictions to development on the land. Australian Capital Territory vendors are also required to provide an energy efficiency rating statement and a pest inspection report (neither of which are required in a Victorian Section 32 document).

Cooling Off Period

Not all buyers have the luxury of a cooling off period, with legislation changing from state to state. During a cooling off period, a buyer can change their mind about purchasing a property and only face a small fee (usually 0.25% of the purchase price, or less), so long as they provide written notice to the vendor or their agent.

In **Victoria**, there is no cooling off period for properties purchased at auction. There is a three-day cooling off period for private sales of residential properties of less than twenty hectares, but this is waived if the property is sold three days before or after a scheduled auction.

The cooling off period is also waived if a buyer is represented by an agent.

The **Australian Capital Territory, New South Wales,** and **Queensland** all have five-day cooling off periods for residential property purchases at private sales, but not for auction sales. Generally, the cooling off period begins from the day that the buyer or their agent receives a copy of the sales contract that has been signed by both the buyer and the seller.

South Australian property sales come with a cooling off period of two days. If a Form 1 is provided before the sale, then the cooling off period commences on the date the contract is signed. If the Form 1 is served after the contract is signed, the cooling off period begins on the day the form is served.

Properties in the **Northern Territory**, which are not sold by auction, come with a cooling off period of four days.

Investors buying in **Western Australia** and **Tasmania** are not allowed cooling off periods.

Stamp Duty Or Land Transfer Tax

Do not forget that stamp duty or land transfer taxes change from state to state, and depend on your property's intended purpose. Each state's revenue office website has a stamp duty calculator that can help you estimate how much you will be charged. **New South Wales** and **Queensland** have strictly enforced transfers by nomination and purchases through an option (puts and calls, as well), leading to the payment of double stamp duty in some cases. Any buyer considering changing the names of the ultimate buyer should be aware that they may be liable for stamp duty costs that were not in their original budget.

Who Can Help?

Purchasing a property interstate can be a difficult task, especially if you are not an experienced investor and you are looking to invest in a state you have not lived in before. The best way to ensure you have all the aspects of your investment covered is to engage a local conveyancer.

As a specialist lawyer, your conveyancer can prepare and lodge your legal documents, such as your contract of sale. They can also calculate your expenses, put your deposit in a trust account, and research the property for you. A conveyancer should also handle your property's settlement, including liaising with your financial institution. As always, seek out a reputable conveyancer, and make sure their firm is not also representing the vendor of the property you are hoping to purchase.

Purchasing interstate is a great way to spread risk across your property's portfolio or capitalise on growth areas – just make sure you do your homework.

Final Word

You have come to the end of my book, and I am sure you have been able to take a great deal of benefit from having read it. There is a considerable amount of information and detail in this book about commercial property, subdivision, development, and conveyancing. However, this information does not replace the services of a suitably qualified and experienced professional; it is general information only, and not legal advice. The most important thing you could take away is to engage the services of a suitably qualified professional. Without these services, I believe many of you will struggle. It may be difficult to grow a portfolio of adequate size to suit your future needs. We have to live life for today, but also live life with tomorrow in mind.

This book should be read in conjunction with my other newly released book, the fourth instalment in the *Made Simple* series, entitled *The 100K Property Investment Plan.*

Property investing is a journey – it should be an enjoyable, stress-free journey. If you want to reduce risk, improve potential, eliminate the stress and time in researching, sourcing, and negotiating on a property, and make money on the property, contact me via the details on the following page.

You may surprise yourself with what you can achieve if you dream big and take action.

Contact

If you would like assistance with buyer advocacy, property advice, or being put in contact with a suitably qualified professional for conveyancing, development, commercial finance, mortgage broking, insurance, financial planning, accounting, or property inspections, then contact me and I will endeavour to assist you.

Additionally, you may wish to purchase one of my first two books for the discounted rate of $14.99 (RRP $24.99):

Property Investing Made Simple

Property Finance Made Simple

If you quote 'discount19' you will receive 5% off of our buyer advocacy or property advisory services.

RESOURCES:

To obtain the 'Investment Readiness Questionnaire,' my *Blueprint to Property Investment Success* ©, and your own research checklist, please visit my website:

www.australianpropertyadvisorygroup.com.au

WEBSITES:

www.propertyinvestingmadesimple.com.au

www.propertyfinancemadesimple.net.au

www.australianpropertyadvisorygroup.com.au

www.the100kpropertyplan.com.au

EMAIL:

advice@australianpropertyadvisorygroup.com.au or
Andrew@apag.com.au

PHONE:

1300 760901

SOCIAL MEDIA:

www.facebook.com/australianpropertyadvisorygroup

www.facebook.com/propertyfinancemadesimple/

www.facebook.com/Propertyinvestingmadesimple/

www.twitter.com/CrossleyAndrew

https://www.linkedin.com/in/andrewccrossley/

Notes

www.ingramcontent.com/pod-product-compliance
Lightning Source LLC
LaVergne TN
LVHW022221200926
848481LV00006B/2068
* 9 7 8 1 9 2 5 8 3 0 7 7 4 *